CRUISE SHIP

A Field Guide to the Curious Crui[...] Cruise

By Ruby Allure

CW00864595

Proofed by Lynda Shea

Disclaimer: the following set of Cruise Ship Creatures are a fictionalised version of many years of cruise ship guest observation, an amalgamation of random characters if you like. The stories are a fictionalised version of the numerous incidents that take place on board on a daily basis.

For all those wonderful people I worked with on ships.

You asked me to create this - so here it is...

I hope it makes you belly laugh as you remember many a bizarre incident!

# CHAPTER 0

## INTRODUCTION

Have you ever been on a cruise or are you considering sailing on a cruise ship? Well if you're a bit of a people watcher then this book will provide some cruising entertainment. Using this field guide you can spend hours fascinated by the numerous 'Cruise Ship Creatures' and breeds that emerge on any given cruise. With that in mind, and with the intention to add a bit of fun to those lovely sea days, here is your perfect opportunity to spot a whole variety of 'Cruise Ship Creatures'. An inspired moment began the process of documenting and grouping the creatures into easily recognisable breeds for the keen-eyed deck explorer to play with.

After an accidental collision with a half-naked old man in leopard skin undies we were underway with potential shippy creatures. The posterial thong-sident provided the first 'Cruise Ship Creatures' title: A 'Leopard Skin Lovely', even though the experience wasn't so lovely because he had a very hairy bottom and particularly skimpy leopard skin knickers. A couple of days later I managed to photograph a guest with a huge bouffant that aligned perfectly with the sun. This type of guest filled me with awe because I could illuminate what was effectively her bun. Illuminated buns were an inspiration to me so I had to share the story with as many people as I could. When I relayed the glowing bun story I called my inspiration a 'Bouffant Banshee', which seemed to strike a chord with many of my colleagues who could visualise her in an instant. A bouffant bonanza ensued, during that cruise we 'spotted' numerous bouffant arrangements.  Whenever we noticed a huge back-combed bouffant then we would say 'Did you spot it?'

'What?'

'A Bouffant Banshee'.

Within my department we were all spotting Cruise Ship Creatures and naming them. Obviously this was a fun cruise safari escapade but there was no consistency within the cruisey creatures because they had never been compiled before. So one day on deck we were spotting quite a variety of cruisy creatures and decided that it would be wonderful to have a decent reference guide to make sure we had spotted them. As you can imagine, I took my inspiration from the hard work of Darwin and divided the 'Cruise Ship Creatures' into breeds and individual cruisey clusters. Please enjoy.

## PART 1

## CHAPTER 1

## THE MORE OBVIOUS CRUISE SHIP CREATURES BREED

When spotting the 'Cruise Ship Creatures', it is worth beginning with those that are obvious and in larger numbers. That way you can start your observations with a sense of success. There is nothing worse than 'Cruise Ship Creature' spotting and not spotting one of the little blighters listed below. The reason the below 'Cruise Ship Creatures' are easy to spot is that they appear pretty much on every cruise and they are the type that gravitate to shippy sailing stays. Some of them may come across as a little negative, yet as with all creatures some have a positive influence and others are a little testing. We can learn from their behaviours and notice common patterns within them. That is the joy of such exploratory escapades!

# CHAPTER 2

## THE 'I HAVE DONE SO MANY CRUISES'

There are plenty of these cruisey creatures around and I find that when I previously hosted Officers' tables the 'I Have Done So Many Cruises' take their opportunity to share every cruise they ever experienced. The conversation often begins with 'When my wife and I started cruising over fifty years ago we went on... One of our favourite cruises takes you to the remotest part of... We prefer cruises that go to places such as.... '

What you find with these lovelies is that they will take every opportunity to tell people how many cruises they have been on. Reciting their extreme cruising adventures makes them feel admired. During the Welcome Aboard Party the conversation will be on an entirely different subject and 'Boom!' suddenly there is a tenuous link that provides perfect opportunity for the 'I Have Done So Many Cruises' to hold court. The best way to utilise this creature is to find out which are the best and the worst cruises they have experienced. Also find out which cruise lines they have enjoyed and others they avoid. This cruisey creature is an asset for your future cruise bookings as long as you don't experience your eyes rolling backwards in your head and drop into an unintended nap after a twenty minute monologue on the time that the Captain collided with the dock in Venice.

# CHAPTER 3

## THE SCOOTER RACERS

The scooter phenomenon demonstrates the evolution of humanity. When I talk about scooters I am not talking about those fun children's scooters. Instead, I am referring to those tank-like devices that have replaced electric wheelchairs. They are the ones that have baskets and can be used to transport all manner of human form over quite a variety of terrain.

When I first returned to ships I was astounded by the number of people who transported themselves on scooters. When it came to life boat drill there was a moment when all the souped-up scooter drivers would arrive at once at the muster station. It was like watching a wall of old Hell's Angels descending on the theatre. It was quite a fearsome sight. A wall of old people, huge people and random people all on scooters driving at one door as though it was a race was terrifying. For some reason I thought there might be a rules of the scooter road. I was wrong. Scooters don't seem to follow any rules, instead it is a free for all and every scooter for themselves. In fact, I had to ask them to park nicely as a couple began ramming each other or nudging the others. Times have changed with scooters; at one time people didn't take them seriously. Suddenly the scooter phenomenon came into vogue. There are all manner of scooter to choose from. In the mature age bracket some carry a sense of kudos by individualising their scooters. I have seen golden flames on the sides and scooters adapted to the mods and rockers styling with numerous mirrors. Maybe that is the way forward, backward and down the stairs. As long as the scooter has bling then it doesn't matter how it is driven.

Some of the strangest scooter moments have included watching a lady reverse out of a lift. After colliding with the door a number of times and watching the door almost close on her, I was about to offer her help but she gave me a certain look that said 'I am doing this!' This is when I learned that many scooter drivers really don't want help. Sometimes when you offer they shout 'I can do it myself!' It was as I was about to ask her if she needed assistance that she suddenly figured the angle out, put her scooter on full reverse throttle and charged backwards down the stairs. She hit the wall, rebounded and went forwards down the next set of stairs. When she arrived on the landing she continued to her destination as though she had planned the manoeuvre. My concern is that as she gains scooter power she will start ram-raiding.

Another example of the extreme scootering caught my attention by the gangway. Ever thought you would witness two people playing chicken on a scooter? Well it seems that once a person gets their super scooter, then they are going to rule the scootering world! They come first and everyone has to respond to them or get out of their way. Their scooter antics make them a scooter of power! This may work for one person but when a few people adopt this scooty attitude then that is when things become dangerous. When I say dangerous we are talking potential carnage. So imagine this: two souped-up scooters both with drivers carrying the same kamikaze attitude. One scooter had flags and streamers while the other was blinged up with gold: gold mirrors, gold plating - gold everything. Both intended to get to the gangway before the other. Both came from opposite directions. Both saw each other and revved their throttles to full speed. An expression of determination combined with flatulence appeared on both of their faces. The old dear had long white hair trailing down her back and the bald old chap wore goggles like those worn by fighter pilots in the 1940s. As the pair gained speed people jumped out of the way while both scooter maniacs put their heads down and focused. It was as though they were involved in some kind of speedway, and guess what happened? It was immaculate because neither was going to beat the other and neither was going to give in. So what happened? They reached the gangway at the same precise moment and collided with each other. 'Boom!' One was thrown from the scooter and the other thrown over the handlebars which kept the throttle moving, pushed the other scooter out of the way and directed her down the corridor. The entire atrium stood in silence and then the miracle happened, the gold scooter driver stood up, got back on his scooter and drove down the gang way a grin. 'I won,' he muttered.

There was also the phantom scooter menace. She had arrived at a point in her life where she simply did not care. She carried a bottle of whisky and drunkenly drove the scooter. Yep drunk and in control of a scooting device. She drove over people's feet and then drove at people. At first she got away with it but then she met a new friend and the pair became extreme. Her new friend was in a wheelchair and what she would do was drive past, he would grab onto the back of her scooter and she would go to full throttle with him clinging on screaming with delight. In one of the ports the pair managed to find a duck sounding hooter. So not only did the pair drive around the ship at full speed quacking, they became menaces to the other guests. There were times when the pair set up ambushes to drive out of random areas at unsuspecting guests. In the end the pair were pulled in and advised they would be disembarked if their behaviour continued. The duck quacking scooter driver sobbed apologetically but on the final day of her cruise she was back to her drunken scooter driving antics. She had one day left and she was going to give it some erratic driving welly!

# CHAPTER 4

## THE WORLD CRUISERS

There is no denying that the 'World Cruisers' are a type. They are an exclusive club of individuals that have enough disposable income to be able to spend between three months to six months a year on a ship. That is quite a lot of disposable income and an enormous amount of available time. Many of the world cruises are over a hundred days. Imagine being able to holiday for over a hundred days per year. There are regular 'World Cruisers' who take world cruises year on year. In fact, when I worked on one of the more exclusive ships (that catered for millionaires and billionaires) there was a woman who had accumulated fourteen years on that specific line. She was in her eighties; however, if you think about it she would have spent at least six months per year cruising over twenty-eight years or alternatively three months per year over fifty-six years. This woman had more time cruising on the ship than most of the crew who worked on the ship. On some ships she had spent more time on board than the Captain. To make her situation increasingly fascinating was that she had arrived at a point where she didn't bother getting off in every port. She said she had been to the places so many times that she did not see the point. What she loved about being on the ship was that she was looked after and served. This makes you understand why there are those, in the elderly bracket, who would prefer to spend the twilight years of their life on a cruise ship rather than stuck in an old people's home.

Back to the world cruising creatures and how to spot them. Quite often the 'World Cruisers' carry or wear branded items from the world cruise revealing a previous world cruise they experienced. They usually have bags that list ship names, previous world cruises and the year. They bring one of those bags for each year that they have taken a world cruise. When you are in the cruise terminal there will be suitcases that have world travel stickers on them, there may even be a hint of Phileas Fogg style suitcasery.

'World Cruisers' usually form a 'Worldie network', a globe-trotting gang if you like, when they arrive on the ship for the world cruise. Usually they know all the staff and the majority of the world cruising guests. When 'World Cruisers' gather they often reflect on the great times, and those times when world cruises have gone terribly wrong. What makes it fascinating is at the time guests were in uproar over storms, missing ports and random events. Had there been any pitch-forks within reach then there would have been numerous casualties. Yet when 'World Cruisers' gather at the beginning of the next world cruise, they reminisce as though the pitch-fork wielding incidents were fond times. They have a tendency to reflect fondly on the time the ship was hijacked by aliens or some other random event with a dreamy expression on their faces. The 'World Cruisers' chuckle and smile about the time a giant octopus emerged from the depths, or the time the ship surfed the Tsunami (please note these are made-up incidents. There have been no actual ship alien abductions that I am aware of). In general the world cruise has between a few hundred and a thousand guests (depending on the size of the ship). Each of those guests can take part in a world circumnavigation voyage for a hundred days or more. Now imagine what that does to people other than enable them to gain a few stone in weight, generate a huge amount of gossip in the launderette and become accustomed to being served on a daily basis. There is of course an increase in the purchase of Panama hats and Pith helmets. Oh I think this leads perfectly into the next cruising creature: the 'Do you know who I Am?'

# CHAPTER 5

## THE 'DO YOU KNOW WHO I AM?'

There are self-important people, there are people who feel they are entitled and there are the 'Do You Know Who I Ams?' of this world. These 'Cruise Ship Creatures' stroll around with a sense of deserving, they often have their noses at a forty-five degree angle and are known to click their fingers to gain a waiter's attention. Most of the time they are harmless until the inner 'Do You Know Who I Am?' rises to the surface. That inner demanding child usually turns up when there is a queue or no places left on a tour. They put on their tweed jacket and riding boots or their best suit to stand at the reception desk or tour desk to make their demands. Some get so irate that they slam their hands down on the desk. When they don't get their way they take a deep breath, their head looks as though it will explode and they then reach for the obvious and tried and tested trick 'Do You Know Who I Am?'

Nope.

Who cares?

You're a dick! That's who you are.

> I love watching the reaction of the person who is on the receiving end of the comment especially when they completely ignore the demands and make no response. Of course the receiving party have heard that little beauty before. Of course the 'Do You Know Who I Ams?' have to pull out all the stops and name drop. Of course they know all the high ranking Officers and all the important people in head office. It never works, it gets boring and even when people do know who they are then selective amnesia is definitely the best course of action. What the 'Do You Know Who I Ams?' don't know is that they are moved to the bottom of the pile because they are annoying. The louder they shout, the more they get in the end... In the meantime, there is satisfaction in knowing that the crew on board are not interested, they are doing a job for everyone. So knowing who someone is doesn't change

that. Oh and sometimes you don't actually want to know who they are.

# CHAPTER 6

## THE READERS

Spending time on a cruise ship, with numerous days at sea, is the 'Reader's' idea of heaven. Nicely lit decks where you can bask in the sun and read that book you have been longing to read but haven't had time is a real joy. You see people with iPads, hardbacks, paperbacks, audiobooks and digital readers dotted around the decks during the day and night. Each 'Reader' seeks a place of solitude to escape into that novel. I will be honest; this is also my idea of heaven. What makes it increasingly ideal for the 'Readers' is that there is usually a library on board and a place that enables book swaps. Lovely eh?

Of course some people can't just read, there are the extreme reading creatures. Yep they are out on deck in storms and rain engrossed in reading that novel. There are some who I have even passed by who sit up by the funnel reading their holiday book. Obviously the idea of getting lost in a book seems to have been misread and interpreted as being lost in a bizarre location with a book. There have even been instances where 'Readers' have been found in some secret nooks and crannies including a cupboard. Yep, a comfy chair, a headlamp and a cupboard space provided the perfect opportunity to escape into a novel. My favourite was a chap who was on deck at 5.30am reading his book. It was 5.30 in the morning and I wondered whether he had been there all night. I would complete my deck walking hour and he would still be there. Later in the day I would do my deck checks and wander past him – he was still there. Later on in the evening guess what? He was still reading. Either he read very slowly or he had numerous books to trawl though. I guessed that he must have developed piles over the twenty-four day cruise. At one point I was concerned that there had been an accident with superglue and he was too embarrassed to ask for help. Just to make sure, I would shake up my routines out of curiosity and the majority of the time he was on deck. He did leave his position for meals and he was gone by 9.00pm because he probably had to sleep. What made the situation intriguing was that he was cruising with his wife and she was nowhere to be seen until the day they departed the ship. He was in his usual place while disembarkation ensued and his wife came and found him. 'Darling, we are going to have to go home.' He looked like a child who had sat on a bee. He loved his reading and his 'special' space. Now he had to leave. Did he finish the book? Who knows?

## CHAPTER 7

## THE LIBRARY LURKERS

The other reading extreme is those who love libraries. Some people just love a library, they like the quiet and a place to retreat and read. On the ship there is usually a special library area for those who like to sniff books, browse shelves and peruse travel guides. It is a place of concentrated knitwear, where silence is appreciated and the leather chairs facing the window enable a sea view whilst reading a long anticipated epic adventure. This type of 'Cruise Ship Creature' is easy to spot because all you need to do is walk past the library and the library lurking breed will have congregated. What does concern me is that there are 'Library Lurkers' who choose to hang out in the library when the ship is in port, even if it is a nice day. I have overheard conversations justifying why they do it: 'I have been on so many cruises and visited so many ports that I am just happy staying on the ship so I can read a good book.' Obviously they could take the book ashore and read on land but that is how you define the purest 'Library Lurkers' because being in the Library with a book beats the adventure of a port.

# CHAPTER 8

## THE SPAGASMICS

'Oh God... Oh my Goooood... I just found the spa and it's SPAAAAAAGASMIC!!!!' Loud breathing followed by a flush of red appearing on the 'Spagasmic's' neck is an indicator or this Spa-loving-shippy creature. This creature loves to spa. They are fresh-faced, everything is waxed and they are so well maintained. They love treatments, they love hydro pools and when it comes to spa demonstrations they are there in the front row. They think nothing of spending a couple of hundred pounds on a facial and they are a delight for the Spa Manager. Actually talking of delights, I think I will provide a few fun stories about the spa marketing campaigns on some of the ships I worked on. To be honest I was horrified that these little mistakes had not been picked up before I fell about the office laughing. In fact, I am astounded that the 'Complainers' did not cause a spa riot.

To give a little insight: every day on the ship there is an equivalent to a newspaper which provides all the activities for the day. On the cover there are adverts for the Casino, the Spa and the Shops etc. Each concession fights for pride of place. It is no surprise that the spa want as much custom as possible and will pull out all the discount tricks to get you up there. There are hot stone massages, reflexology and all kinds of hair seminar. Each of these is supposed to have a catchy phrase to draw you in... As an example - LOSE EIGHT INCHES (off what?) Come to this spa talk and watch eight inches disappear. I can tell you now that not many men would attend that talk because most would end up in an inch-loss deficit.

FACIALS CAN BE FUN... (You can't really smile or talk) Come and learn about the fun found in facials. This insightful talk will detail how to combat wrinkles, fine lines and facial fat. (Were they going to teach people unarmed facial combat?)

Then came a shocker 'OUR SOLE DELIGHT'. Say that little beauty slowly and you might get away with it. Now say it aloud with a bit of speed and then see how it sounds... Oh I fell about laughing when I noticed that. Of course I phoned the spa and asked whether the 'Our Sole Delight' was an anus massage or maybe it was a Vajazzle for anal orifices. Well I soon learned it was simply a foot massage. When I made the spa receptionist say 'Our Sole Delight' down the phone she did not get it. In the end I had to explain that an English person may well be a little concerned by someone delighting in their arsehole. It was beyond them. After that first delightful marketing insight I thought I should keep my eyes trained on the spa marketing wording. A few weeks later this little beauty rose to the surface: FUN AND FASCINATING FACIALS. *Enjoy this relaxing facial which tones, detoxifies, moisturises and builds to the most wonderful decapitation. Your face will look fresh, revived and be the talk of the ship.*

Your face will definitely be the talk of the ship if it is not attached to your body. Out of courtesy I thought I would chat with the Spa Manager.

*'So this Fun and Fascinating Facial.... You can't get much repeat custom...'*

*'We aren't getting any custom.'*

*'I am not surprised.'*

*'Why?'*

*'Well why would you go for a facial that builds up to having your head cut off?'*

*The Spa Manager was quiet as she tried to comprehend.*

*'Read the advert that you sent me.'*

*She read it and remained silent. 'I don't get it.'*

*'Well the treatment ends in a decapitation. I am sure that is not what you wanted to say.'*

*'Ohhhhhh shit! It is meant to say exfoliation.'*

*There are obviously a few of these beauties but I will end with this little number:*

*WE GIVE HEAD AND LOVE FEET. PLUS ENJOY A LITTLE SURPRISE. Come experience a wonderful Indian head massage, followed by a foot massage. Free eye with every treatment.*

Now that is a surprise... Well there are few things that are a little questionable... I guess you figured it out. How on earth do you honour a free eye with every treatment? What a surprise! 'Madam don't forget your free eye!'

So again I called the Spa Manager, who by this point rolled her eyes (possibly the free give away eyes) every time she heard I was on the phone.

'Hello... so how do I get my free eye?'

'What do you mean?'

'Well there is a free eye with every treatment. Is it a human eye? Or if it is an animal eye then I think you might offend vegetarians and vegans. I would probably find out whether people are vegetarian or vegan before they have the treatment and maybe give them a sprout instead of the eye. I don't think they would like eyes...'

There was a confused silence from the Spa Manager, who was from a remote part of Europe.

'I think you should read your advert,' I suggested.

She read it and I sensed she shrugged, she could not see the issue.

'I don't understand.'

'Okay here is what the advert says – you give head – that suggests the spa provides oral sex as a treatment.'

She gasped.

'You don't do you?'

'No of course not... It is meant to say head massages.'

'Ah you forgot a key word then.'

'I don't understand the free eye for the vegetarians.' She read the advert again and whispered 'No...' You could sense her shame. 'Oh I am sorry, it was meant to say eye treatment.'

'I thought so.'

'Did this advert go out like this?'

'Nope that is why I am calling. You may have had good business but I didn't think it was fair on the spa staff since the average age on this cruise is seventy-two. If WE GIVE HEAD AND LOVE FEET. PLUS ENJOY A LITTLE SURPRISE, had been advertised you would be expected to honour it.'

She breathed a sigh of relief. 'Thank you.'

All in all the spa provides many a treatment, they might not know what they are offering but that is not the point. It is a wonderful place to visit and you too could become SPAGASMIC with the right treatment.

CHAPTER 9

THE 'BEEN THERE DONE IT AND AM WEARING THE T-SHIRT, HAVE
THE MAGNETS AND WEAR A BASEBALL CAP WITH THE LOCATION ON
IT – JUST IN CASE YOU MISSED WHERE I HAVE TRAVELLED TO'


This type of passenger is similar to the 'We Have Been On So Many
Cruises' creatures but there is actually a subtle difference. These
guests don't need to make a huge noise about where they have been
instead they have numerous items of clothes that clearly show
where they have been. So for example, if they walked over the
Sydney Harbour Bridge then they will have a t-shirt or a sweatshirt
with 'Sydney Harbour Bridge' written in big letters. If they went cage
diving with great white sharks in South Africa there will probably be
a baseball cap with a shark's head emerging from it with 'I survived
the sharks,' and the location. Alternatively, they may have purchased
the swimming hat with the shark fin on to terrorise the guests in the
pool. Of course that shark fin swimming hat will have the location on
so that people can ask questions. If you think about it these guests
are pretty clever because they wear clothes that can initiate
conversations. When they are in port they will hunt for that special
clothing item and the 'bloody magnet' to put on their fridge. Later
that evening they will bring that magnet to the dining table to show
everyone what they have found.

Okay while I am on the subject of magnets. I cannot get over how
many people collect travel magnets. I am sure that some people's
fridges must run out of magnet space. Maybe they buy an additional
fridge to increase the display. If a crew member can't get ashore,
then they ask a colleague to purchase a magnet from that location. It
is the same when some of the guests are ill or don't want to go
ashore, they often ask other guests to go magnet hunting for them. I
never understood the whole magnet thing until I went to one of the
Officer's cabins for a party, and since the wall was metal, there were

21

magnets adorning it from pretty much every port in the world. He had a map at the centre of that wall and it was amazing to see all the places he had visited. Small pieces of red string connected the pins to the appropriate magnet. This wasn't the only fascinating thing; he also had an entire mini-garden and was growing his own chillies. Amazing eh? Who would have guessed what can grow next to a port hole.

Oh and back to this particular 'Cruise Ship Creature', you often won't find them mixing with the 'We Have Done So Many Cruises' because the conversation becomes competitive. This 'Cruise Ship Creature' would rather display numerous clothing items that will suggest how many places they have visited and what their favourite places are throughout the cruise. These creature types are usually pretty fun and will know the best places to buy the souvenirs. What's more, they will be able to assist you in future cruises and if you are into the more exciting tours, they will advise you what it is like to look a great white shark in the eyes and not get eaten. If they advise you to wear a swimming hat with a shark fin, then maybe they are winding you up! Oh and this type of 'Cruise Ship Creature' could also cross-breed and be witnessed in the 'More Showy Types' of 'Cruise Ship Creature' Breed. As I mentioned before, we are going for those cruisey creatures that are easy to spot first to get ourselves visually warmed up for some more exciting, dangerous and rare breeds of 'Cruise Ship Creature' further into the field guide.

# CHAPTER 10

## THE SHOPAHOLICS – AND THE CLEARANCE SALE CHARGE

Some people just love a bargain and even better, when there is a sea day and feel a need for activity, what better way to spend your time than battling others for that elusive ship's cat key ring or a sparkly piece of junk jewellery that has fifty percent off? Of course there is also the option to purchase reduced price Captain's hats so you can join the Captain's Hat brigade. If a guest is lucky then they could buy two for the price of one. These fresh Captain's hats could become the 'His' and 'Hers' of the Captain's hat creature kind. That means both he and she can parade about the deck in reduced priced Captain's hats with that smug grin that accompanies a bargain.

Now it seems that something strange happens to people's sense of style on the ship. Maybe it is because people don't know each other, so they can be more experimental with pattern combinations or wear something they would never usually wear, such as kilts. I was somewhat amazed when the ship stocked kilts after a visit to Scotland. Obviously they were only really appealing for a short duration of time on the Scotland cruise. Unfortunately, the Shop Manager had been overly optimistic about kilt selling potential and over-ordered. During the following cruise to Norway the kilts went on sale. That formal night there was an increase in men who had never been to Scotland, had no relatives in Scotland, wearing kilts. There was a strange understanding amongst them: first they had a bargain, second they got to wear a kilt which was airy around their fairy, and third when else would they wear a kilt for no real reason? Such circumstances reveal the true power of a tartan bargain.

# CHAPTER 11

## THE SOCKS AND SANDALS BRIGADE

At the moment I am thinking of odd tan lines. This then made me ask the question: Why do people wear long socks and sandals? Actually a better question is: Why do men reach a certain age and think that socky sandaldom is a good idea? Is there a mysterious moment where a sandal and sock gene is triggered which drives a man to wear such sockacious abominations? Is there a coincidental moment where that same man develops the capacity to 'dad dance' and embarrass all of those who surround him? Well it seems that blokes of a 'Sock and Sandals' brigade flock together, especially on cruises. There may even be the potential for a sandal and sock off. The average sandal-socker is likely to wear beige or off-white socks and brown leather sandals. They are the least adventurous of the sock-tastic gang; however, there are the more shockingly adventurous who will wear patterned knee-high socks and the equivalent of an 'off road 4X4' sandal. It is as if they are taunting their sandalatious sockington hierarchy and tainting their footwear with a hint of danger and adventure. Maybe there is an alpha sockacious sandal wearing male that dominates the others simply by the colour and positioning of sock to intensity of sandal grip ratio. You know that there is further challenge when the socks and sandals are teamed with a leather hat. The 'Socks and Sandals' brigade are an obvious 'Cruise Ship Creature': most wear the standard chino shorts, white shirts or t-shirts and the socks and sandals. They almost get away with it. Yet once you have identified the usual socky-sandal offenders then it is time to refine the socky-sandal spotting because there are rarer breeds within the 'Socks and Sandals' brigade. There are those who wear long socks and sandals with budgie smugglers (small swimming trunks) who knows why anyone thinks that is a good idea.  There are those, and these are the rarest, socks and sandals with a sarong. If you see one of those then you have probably witnessed one of the most unique socky-sandal creature within the group. If you do witness one of these phenomenon then I

24

suggest you learn to believe in miracles too because that is a truly great spotting, almost like seeing an albino white tiger wearing stilettos.

# CHAPTER 12

## THE SHIP'S NAPPER

Have you ever considered all the different places that can be napped on a cruise ship? When you are on holiday there is every opportunity to nap with no judgement by fellow cruisers. In my humble napping opinion, luxury cruises should definitely involve some sea day luxury napping. There is nowhere to go during a sea day so one can take an opportunity to nap whenever they please. Also that cruising holiday has been earned and most definitely the luxury of a nap is part of true rest and recuperation without repercussion. So when it comes to napping there are obvious places to take a nap like on the deck in the sun, by the pool and in some of the quieter lounges. Yet there is a different league of napper who can take napping to the extreme, in fact I have witnessed some rather fantastic napping phenomenon. My amusement can never be concealed when there are nappers who nap on the front row of lectures. What makes it all the more amusing is a loud snore and a grunt when the lecturer passionately discloses a deeply insightful fact. Nappers combined with knitters could really destroy a lecturer's confidence.

Imagine the most flamboyant show with glitz, glamour, can cans and acrobatics, and at a crucial moment a loud snore dominates the theatre. Even worse when there are a number of naughty nappers snoring in unison or out of synch. The sound can be likened to a chainsaw combined with mating walruses. You might think that I am joking but it does actually happen. I remember one particular cast being absolutely devastated when they glanced at the front row of theatre and about ten people were having a nap. At least they weren't dead! Or maybe they were – the dancing entertainment may have overwhelmed.

After noticing numerous napping tactics, I came to the conclusion there are purposely aggravating nappers who find the most inconvenient places to nap. So when there are groups playing Bridge (in the bridge room). An opportunist napper can snore while the players try and focus on their game.

The ballroom dancing seems to draw a number of nappers to sit on seats and nap. My favourite is when Caribbean night is taking place and all the entertainment staff are giving it some welly and there are a cluster of nappers sitting in front of them. The music can be loud, the entertainment team can dance but a naughty napper will simply keep nodding forward, grunt, and return to their original position.

Oh the joy of napping and the joy of naughty napping.

# CHAPTER 13

## THE WELL-KNOWN WHINGERS AND THE CONSTANT COMPLAINERS...
## THERE IS A LIST

What people don't know is that most cruise lines keep a list of the 'Constant Complainers' and the 'Well-known Whingers'. Every time the whinger complains it is recorded and compiled. In addition, the amount of compensation that is paid to them per whine is added to the list. Fascinating eh? When certain people reach a certain level of complainership the cruise line can actually refuse for them to sail on their ship or any of their sister ships or companies under the same umbrella. Obviously they do this politely at first.

So one day we were preparing for the next cruise and having a look at the notorious ones who were about to embark. It was as if all the extreme complainers had all decided to cruise together. Now these people have a plan. They arrive on the ship and their minds are focused on finding fault. Anything from a toilet blockage to a tissue on the floor will trigger them. Quite often they photograph ship faults using their phones. Rather than enjoy the cruise they are set on getting money back. What a shame eh? The thing is we all do our best to avoid being stuck with these people because not only will they launch into a monologue about why they will never sail with that particular ship again, they will tell you why other companies are better. Also they will then make demands for free everything. There is an amazing sense of entitlement. These people rile people up and create riots. It is an embarrassment but it seems that their focus is to share their discontent. When it comes to hosting the Officer's table there is nothing worse than being stuck on a table for two hours with those who find fault. I once had one of these challenging tables and was at the end of my contract, so had absolutely no tolerance. During one particular rant, I stopped them mid-flow because I had

had enough and said 'Stop! Now the way I see it is if you shine a torch on a turd you get an illuminated turd. I don't like having my attention focused on glowing turds.' There was a stunned silence because you don't use the word turd at dinner or in polite society but I was hardly going to use the word shit. Once I had their attention I continued, 'I would like you all to take your mental torches and shine it on something nice otherwise I will have to excuse myself from this table.' After a few people muttered 'An illuminated turd?' under their breaths, one of them began to laugh and so did the others. The mentality amongst the group did actually shift; however, I expected to have some major personal complaints after being so abrupt. What was amazing was that it did not happen; instead, I was surprised to be thanked for breaking a spiral of negativity. The thing with complaining is that it does not actually change anything. One needs to talk to the source of the aggravation directly otherwise what the complainer is doing is aggravating everyone and expecting another person to go to the source of the issue. Of course there are cases where a person does need to complain – for example if your cabin is filled with bedbugs, the ship's toilets are blocked or a pipe bursts while you are asleep. The difference is those who search for issues to complain about rather than those who end up in awkward circumstances. It is easy to identify the 'Constant Complainers' because they will appear as though they have a smell under their nose and will often look like they are inspecting the ship. If you ever feel the urge to be really annoying and fancy giving them something to complain about then smile at them kindly and say: 'Turn that frown upside down!' Ha!

# CHAPTER 14

## THE FAMILIES

Some ships are purposely set up for 'Families'. They have climbing walls, super-fast slides, ice rinks and all manner of playground entertainment especially for the little kiddie-winkies. There are specific youth workers who are employed to entertain the children and provide fun activities. Sometimes the youngsters go on treasure hunts, other times they play Giant Jenga or they get to make huge papier-mache sculptures. On some ships there are children-friendly swimming pools that keep the little dudes away from those who are not family favourers. In some cases, parents arrive on board, drop their kids off at the pool (the swimming pool with the youth workers) and behave as though they are childless. During the evening the children remember they have parents because they have their dinner with them.

Christmas is a major time for 'Families' on ships where you can have up to five generations of a family in a confined space for two weeks. Now that is a dynamic to witness especially when Great Granny Mable gets wasted and races around the ship on her scooter, often with a couple of grandkids on her lap. When these kind of antics unfold there are usually repercussions and there are times when a whole family erupts into cruise conflict. It usually happens at sea, during a storm, when the children are spewing, the parents haven't slept and granny has just attended the single's party and returned with her new beau. Fabulous eh? For the most part 'Families' appear happy because there is plenty of food choice and entertainment but there are times when you wonder whether one of the older matriarchs may well disappear overboard by the end of the cruise. 'Missing in extreme scooter action.'

# CHAPTER 15

## THE SINGLES, THE MINGLES AND THE DESPERATE

There seems to be a myth that when you are single and go on a cruise ship that you will meet the love of your life. There are times when two singles magnetically gravitate to each other; however, the reality is there are usually a lot more single women than men, it is likely due to the fact that when single men go on the ship there is a full stampede of elderly and available ladies in their direction. Within that stampede, which resembles scenes from 'Black Friday,' there is all manner of body slamming, hair pulling and wig tossing in an effort to reach the man before the others. That is quite a trauma for an unsuspecting sandal and sock wearer who innocently thought he would be able to watch exotic sea birds rather than be mowed down by a flock of old-dear-birds.

Of course it isn't always like that and there are singles parties. I have attended these both in the capacity as an Officer (where I had to chat with single guests) and in previous years as a photographer. The first singles party I attended was an eye-opener because the age group on the ship appeared to be eighty plus. The entertainment staff had rounded up the singles, provided them with 'singles hats' which were silver, encrusted in glitter and had a red heart above the rim. In addition, a red heart badge was given to the group. I found it amusing how readily accepted the adornments were. Then the jaw dropping moment evolved when the group were arranged in lines: man, woman, man, woman... They were then handed an orange and were advised that each group had to pass the orange to the end of the line. What made it all the more exciting was that they had to pass it neck to neck. Once the orange made it to its final destination un-squeezed, they then had to pass a balloon from legs to legs. It was an amazing sight to watch people in their eighties and nineties get so balloonily involved.

When that little game was complete the group were then enticed into gyrating and dancing which resulted in a Macarena dance. I stood shaking my head in amazement – you couldn't pay for such entertainment. Finally, the group had to pass a key attached to a string down the women's tops and down the men's trousers. It was one of those moments where you wonder whether you are caught up in a weird nightmare or a joke. Of course it was a bonding moment and yes it seemed to work. A few of the singles mingled and paired up throughout the cruise, which was very sweet.

There are of course the single Officer hunters as well. These are ladies who come on board with the intention to hide the sausage with an Officer or try and go a step further and find one to marry. What most have no idea about is that there are only a certain number of Officers and most are already married. NOTE: THERE IS MORE ABOUT THIS PARTICULAR CREATURE FURTHER INTO THE BOOK. Another thing they don't know is that every cruise there is a new batch of Officer hunters. On top of that, the women who work on board intend to get together with an Officer because they have their own cabins and don't have to share. So with all that in mind, those Officers in their uniforms are in demand. Of course there are those with morals, values and commitment. There are those that view every porthole as a sausage-hiding goal. So the Officer hunters are a wonderful group to watch because when you are on board for months at a time there is the chance to run an 'Officers who have been hunted tally' where the ladies who hunt believe they have achieved something spectacular when in fact they are just a number on a sea-sausagey treadmill. That isn't being nasty, it is the reality. I knew one Security Officer who had a wife on land, a 'ship wife', a ship girlfriend, women in most ports, and was still on the lookout for more opportunity. He was pretty greedy or some might say sex glutinous and liked sexploration. When I asked him how he justified himself he said they all knew, they all accepted it and it was a case that being a red-blooded man he needed to keep oil in the engine. Admittedly he was honest and he advised all the ladies involved. He said that by having that approach then it was up to them to make

32

their decision based on the circumstances. It seemed that most were curious and when someone is in demand, well that makes them increasingly desirable.

There is another set of singles: the 'Desperate'. Since all singles are not the same and sometimes there are those needy and desperate souls who make a reputation for themselves. There have been times where the 'Desperate' make a nuisance of themselves by harassing staff or stalking potential lovers. What makes it ever so enthralling is the tactics that they employ. Room service is an obvious 'draw a person to the room' technique. Then there are those who 'lurk' in accessible areas or hover by the crews' sun deck. There are older women who offer cash to room stewards for services above and beyond. There are chaps who make lude suggestions and ask for the spa massage to have a 'happy ending.' The stories you hear in the crew bar and Officers' wardroom would make your jaw drop. What you do learn is that all manner of pervaciousness occurs when people are desperate. The problem is that through being friendly and serving, the crew's behaviour can be misconstrued. If a person has been lonely for a while, people actively having a conversation with them can suggest interest. There have been times when the 'Desperate' have crossed boundaries which has resulted in complaints involving the Captain. If someone is abused by a passenger and there are witnesses and evidence, then that passenger can be disembarked in the next port. That is satisfying to know when you are a crew member and not so impressive when you are a 'Desperate'.

CHAPTER 16

## THE SUN WHACKY WORSHIPPERS

Have you ever noticed the human prune? These people have tanned so hard that they are the darkest shade of leather. When they stand up and their bikini bottoms or trunks slip the contrast is astounding. The other example of this creature is the barbecued version where they bask in the sun far too long that they reach a red so deep that it resembles blood. They have gone beyond lobster to something far more disturbing. What always astounds me is that even though they are burned, they will go back out the next day and the next day and repeat until they shed skin like dandruff imbued snakes. Of course there are some sub-species of the 'Sun Whacky Worshippers' and these are detailed below.

The Leathery Sunbathers: okay this title can be interpreted in two ways. There are people that sunbathe in leather. Oh yes, on a charter cruise for gay men, it seemed that some would venture out on deck in their leather 'swimwear' and tan themselves. Some would even wear the leather hat and chains. I have no idea what they do with tan lines or whether these lines were part of the 'kink'. On non-charter cruises, the leather-clad chain wearer is a very rare breed of 'Cruise Ship Creature'. However, the gay charter cruises are always a laugh, will open your mind and at times make you wonder how on earth 'that (insert random object) got stuck in that hole.'

While we are on the subject of charter cruises I guess that you would be surprised that there are in fact nudist charters where the guests are naked. There is a more detailed insight further into the field guide on this type of 'Cruise Ship Creature'.

Soooo back to the actual 'Leathery Sunbathers' – these are the people that are so brown and so tanned that their skin is like leather. They are easy to spot because they are soooo soooo brown. When you glimpse a tan line you will be astounded by their original skin state. Beneath all that tan there was once a pale and very pasty skin. For the extreme 'Sun Whacky Worshipers' there is kudos in sunbaking. Many go on cruises for the extreme tans to show off when they return to England in the middle of the winter. These people tend to wear lighter clothes the browner they get and by the time they are super tanned, have you noticed they all suddenly wear white? When they arrive back to the Southampton gloom, these people still maintain their white and wafty outfits even if it is minus twelve. No matter what, they have to show off that tan as they make their way home. Why would you put in all that tanning effort if you can't show it off?

# CHAPTER 17

## THE SUNBED HOGGERS

Over the years there have been many jokes about the Germans hogging sunbeds. Well I am glad to inform you that sunbed hogging is not nation specific. It seems that if there is a sunbed in the near vicinity then an 'International Hogger' will be called to action and often in the most extreme states of hoggaciousness. The potential 'Sunbed Hogger' has a certain sixth sense for discovering a free and very desirable sunbed.

Sometimes, when making my deck-checking rounds of the ship at 5.30am or 6.00am, a miracle had already taken place. The reason that I call it a miracle is that the staff who put out the sun loungers couldn't even work out how the 'Hoggers' managed to mark their hoggy territory without detection. There must have been some very clever disguises or camouflage being used. As soon as a sun lounger touched the deck, and the sun lounger placing crew member turned their back, a towel magically attached itself to the sun lounger along with two pegs to stop that beach towel blowing away. The towel to pegging process took less than five seconds and the phantom 'Hogger' evaporated in to thin cruisey air. It was only when the sun reached its body burning peak that the phantom 'Hogger' would materialise, as if they had been there all the time. Maybe the 'Hoggers' have capes of invisibility too. Of course there were all manner of clever techniques to stop the towels being removed. One of the most inventive involved a blow up doll, a blanket and a number of pegs to stop the blow up doll blowing off. Imagine a giant whoopee cushion in human form flying across the deck making a huge raspberry noise. Why does that amuse me so? Another arranged towels in a body-like form, put a fur hat at the 'head end' and placed a blanket over the top. On top of the blanket a 'Do Not Disturb' sign was fastened so that people would not dare to prod them. Clever? Inventive? There is often quite a lot of creative

36

strategy involved in the most inventive sun lounger hogging techniques. 'Watch and learn!'

# CHAPTER 18

## THE WHITE HATTERS

After all that excitement with the 'Sunbed Hoggers' it is worth taking in some of the gentler 'Cruise Ship Creatures': The White Hatters. Talking of random attire, what is it with all the people who wear white hats? The moment you step on certain cruise ships it is as if an announcement has been made demanding that guests place a shapeless white hat on their heads. These aren't your average hats either instead they look like flimsy buckets made of white material. It is as if Mister Whippy has invented a hat and passengers are just human cornets to transport them. I wonder whether the white hats are the evolution of white handkerchiefs that appeared frequently in 1940s style cartoons of the British on the beach. One fascinating observation is that before the passengers embark the ship there are no white hats and then as soon as they step on board then something happens: the hatty white adornments suddenly appear. Maybe as they pass through the security someone sneakily pops the white hats on their heads.

# CHAPTER 19

## THE REST HOME LOVELIES

'Why go to a rest home when you can pay less and go on a cruise?' That was what one elderly couple said to explain why they spent so many months on the ship. They had booked for the year and could completely justify their time on board. They looked at it like this:

The ship provides you with food, travel and service. You don't have to do housework, you can have your clothes washed and the crew are paid to talk to you, they are increasingly friendly when they receive tips. There are all kinds of food, there are no heating bills and if you want to go and visit a place then transport is laid on for you. If you are ill then there is a ship's doctor. If you die there is a morgue. You are surrounded by people of a similar age and a similar interest, so why sit in a rest home rotting when it is cheaper to travel the world and be looked after? Good point? Rest homes at sea? The other couples on the table agreed and intended to follow suit. What was lovely was that there were numerous single old ladies who were having the time of their lives dancing with gentleman hosts, gossiping in the launderettes and learning advanced techniques in how to play pass the orange. What more could you want when the end is nigh?

# CHAPTER 20

## THE 'WE ONLY CAME ON THIS CRUISE FOR THE PORT WE MISSED'

What people often forget is that the brochure pictures are manipulated and that the dreamy destination images are not actual reality. The truth is cruises are subject to weather conditions, unforeseen events (such as a whale impaling itself on the front of the ship – yes that has happened) and medical emergencies. Some of the random anomaly can be so extreme that the ship will have to change course and unfortunately there are times when ports are missed. The worst case scenario resulted in the ship turning back to its embarkation port. Extreme weather, acts of God or technical difficulties can't be helped – it is the reality of shipping life. As an example: a huge storm erupted in the Mediterranean one October which meant that the ship did not reach Venice. Obviously many of the guests had picked that specific cruise based on that particular port; however, things got worse because not only did the ship not make it into Venice, it didn't make it into Kotor or Corfu. The storm raged and so did the guests: an image of angry human ping-pong balls being flung around reception sprung to mind. That unfortunate sequence of events meant that the majority of the ports on the itinerary were missed. You can understand the disappointment, and when you see passengers crying in public spaces when the Captain makes the port-missing announcement, it just goes to show how important the ports are to the guests.

The cruise best forgotten was when the ship sailed into a number of hurricanes which resulted in the ship missing over five ports out of the ten ports on that cruise. That cruise had fourteen extremely bumpy days at sea over the whole cruise. The usual comment of: 'We only came on this cruise for... (fill in the name of port)' took on a whole new level. At one point there was almost a riot. The Captain was new to his full Captainy role and during the delivery of his announcement it was quite apparent that he had clearly had enough. At the end of the cruise, when it came to the Captain's question time, there was an onslaught of comments. At the end of the interview there was a questions and answers session 'How do you feel about being a shit Captain with a shit team?' one guest asked. The riled-up-guest-filled-theatre became increasingly aggravated and anarchy broke out. As a result, the Captain walked off the stage. It is times like that you understand why companies pay Captains so much money. They have to make decisions based on the safety of the ship and crew. The reason the ship could not make it into the ports was because the winds were so strong that the ship could be blown against the harbour walls. Rather than risk a collision and potential sinking it was safer to remain at sea. Of course the repercussions for the Officers who hosted the Officer's tables at the end of the cruise resulted in numerous references to that infamous phrase: 'We only came on this cruise for...' There was no way I could use the 'If you shine your torch on a turd, you get an illuminated turd' line.

On another ship there was a Captain nicknamed Captain Wimpy by the guests because at any opportunity he would avoid challenging ship parking conditions. What made it worse was some of the ports that he avoided would be filled with at least three other cruise liners who had made it into port without a problem. He would make his apology over the tannoy and the regular cruising guests would go, 'Oh here we go again Captain Wimpy and his excuses.'

Life on board a ship is fascinating because you witness extremes. There is the extreme of 'self' where you have to be polite to people who can be complete arse holes. You have to smile politely when you would rather slap them. There is the extreme inner endurance to continue to work in all conditions and ridiculous hours. Imagine sitting on your work chair which happens to have wheels (not very clever) as the ship rocks back and forth. Hours of rolling away from the desk and then being flung at the desk ensue. Try typing and focusing with those conditions. Work in motion anyone?

For the guests there is extreme gut capacity endurance as they consume more food than their bodies can manage. There are the weather extremes. When the weather is beautiful, there are dolphins off the bow and everyone is relaxed and in a state of bliss. Then there are those times when the weather is erratic and there are huge seas. People bounce off walls, passengers cling to bannisters and the buffet line becomes a buffet bundle. It is when the white pick and mix bags appear around the ship you know that it is going to get rough. Ports are missed and there is clear disappointment. Since there is no way one can control the weather, sea conditions or technical events then all of those potential situations have to be accepted and if you are only going on a cruise to visit a specific port, it might actually be better to go on holiday to that destination because there is no point going on a cruise just to say 'I only came on this cruise for...' Go on the cruise to enjoy the whole cruise and not one specific destination. The way I see it is that when a mass of guests go on a cruise for a specific port then divine humour will of course re-divert the cruise or change it for their own diviney entertainment. That is just how Neptune and his mischievous mates are having a giggle.

PART 2

CHAPTER 21

THE MORE EXCITING CRUISE SHIP CREATURES

To spice things up it is worth searching out the more exotic 'Cruise Ship Creatures'. This section is for those of you who would enjoy spotting cruisey creatures who will amuse you, bemuse and at times enthuse you.

CHAPTER 22

THE LEOPARD PRINT LOVELIES

What is it about the desire to suddenly adorn one's self with leopard skin print and gold lame as soon as one steps on the gangway? I have never figured out the baffling conundrum but these 'Leopard Print Lovelies' must think 'Ah we are going on a cruise - I had best pack all my leopard print outfits.' I have been astounded by the fact that women in their eighties adorn a leopard skin visor, leopard skin bikinis with leopard skin tops and leggings. Their pumps are usually matching or they wear gold sandals and when they take those sandally beauties off then there is even leopard skin print on the inside of that sandal. Amazing! There must be a shop somewhere that rejoices in leopard skin cruising season.

At first I thought it was just a woman thing; however, one evening, in a post work daze, I strolled along a corridor. It was the final night of the cruise and I was not looking where I was going. Unfortunately, an older gentleman, in his late seventies, was bending over his suitcase.

I fell over the top of him. If that was not bad enough, he was not wearing much other than a leopard skin thong and he was putting out his leopard skin suitcase. Obviously there was quite a commotion and his wife opened the cabin door wearing a leopard skin negligee with pink rollers in her hair. It was one of those very surreal moments where an old man in a leopard skin thong offers his hand to help you up while the budgie being smuggled had been eaten by the leopard making up that thong.

# CHAPTER 23

## THE PLASTIC SURGERY EXPERIMENTS

When I first noticed the 'Plastic Surgery Experiments' I wondered whether they had specifically asked the consultant whether they could maintain a continual expression of surprise. Those thoughts then spiralled into 'maybe they want to appear as though they have recently experienced g-force.' Maybe there was some kudos in looking as though you had just experienced a light-speed flight and your face had not returned to its original position yet. I know that may sound cruel; however, I first noticed the phenomenon on one of the more exclusive cruise ships. I literally almost jumped backwards one day when an extremely surprised expression made its way along the corridor. In an effort to 'style out' my response I appeared as though I was warming up for exercise. Yep. It wasn't convincing and the lady who I reacted to didn't smile because it seemed her face was too tight to adjust her mouth from the pout. It turned out that she was a lovely lady too and that her husband was a plastic surgeon. That rang alarm bells for me. 'Darling, I have a new facial arrangement I would like to try out. You fancy it?'
'Of course darling!!!'

Now what struck me as strange is that when I attended cocktail parties on that particular ship there were discussions about who had had what done and by which plastic surgeon. It was a whole new world to me. Some of the 'Plastic Surgery Experiments' went on cruises, stuffed their faces and then had the fat sucked out or redirected to their bottoms or bosoms. Then there were the hair grafters of the male kind. Something about them reminded me of when I was young and had dolls with sprouts of hair, meaning hair sprouting out of their heads in little tuffs. At first I did not understand why a chap would do such a thing to their head until I saw a bald chap walking around the deck and his 'toupee' blew off. When I say blew off I don't mean that it passed wind, I mean it lifted into the air by the means of wind. One minute he had a head full of

45

hair, the next he didn't. A moment later an unsuspecting reader had a flying muff land in her lap. Oh and did she scream. She thought it was a wild creature. She threw it off her lap and then stamped on it. It was a beautiful set of circumstances that provided enlightenment as to why someone would have hair grafted to their head. Can you imagine the humiliation of walking up to a stranger and asking for your wig back?

# CHAPTER 24

## THE TALENT FOR THE NOT SO TALENTED SHOW

Admittedly I love cringe-worthy moments where you just want to curl up and pull an expression like you just bit the inside of your cheek. This is where the ship's talent show really provides the perfect opportunity to be amazed by some people's innate gifts and others dumfounding lack of ability. Before I go any further, there are some amazing talents. There are those who have burst into opera, people who have professed to be stand-up comics and actually made the room laugh. There were a group of ladies who could imitate all kinds of animals and were particularly good at warbling… Amazing imagine sitting watching three seventy year olds warble at the top of their lungs and then break into walrus mating calls. So I am not dismissing that there are talented people out there who love to share their talent with the rest of the ship. Yet it is the ones who are deluded that provide the best entertainment. Take for example the rather portly lady who appeared as though she had sprayed aluminium foil onto her body and proceeded to tap dance, belly dance, gyrate and slap her bottom to what appeared to be a completely different song to that which was playing. When one glanced around the audience the amount of flabbergasted expressions could be likened to over a thousand people unexpectedly experiencing the moment when a bungy jumper made a leap!

What makes the talent show more exhilarating is that the theatre is at the front of the ship and the talent show generally takes place during sea days. Have you figured it out why it gets more exciting? Oh when you have a storm the whole show becomes tremendously thrilling.  The hours of dance choreography goes out of the window when the talent is launched diagonally across the stage but of course the show must go on, even if one of the singers projectile vomits during an emotional crescendo. Imagine an audience clinging to their seats, as they experience a bumpy ride, and a man wielding a sock puppet makes his way onto the stage to perform his ventriloquism act. Now I had never considered how difficult it is to be a ventriloquist with a sock puppet on a stage that is rising, falling and shaking. So this expression of talent was quite a spectacle because have you noticed that when you fall forwards or backwards you often open your mouth? So the whole talking without moving lips issue was elevated to a whole new scale. In the end it turned out that the sock was mute, no matter how much the ventriloquist attempted to lure it into conversation. That sock wasn't going to play the game.

# CHAPTER 25

## THE PARTY CRUISERS

In the cruise industry there are four day cruises that are known to the crew as 'the party cruises.' The reason that these are the party cruises is that the passengers are a type. They are often drinkers who like to party and four days is within their budget to get completely and absolutely smashed. The party cruises that leave from England often go to Amsterdam and have an overnight in the city where cake can cause hallucinations and it is legal to be illegal. The other party cruises sometimes go to Hamburg, Belgium or Guernsey. Those that go from the U.S often visit a few Caribbean islands and involve a huge amount of rum.

Originally the short cruises were designed as taster cruises for those who had never cruised before. They were cheaper and people could get a taste for cruising to see if they wanted to experience longer cruise durations. What the companies had not anticipated was the influx of stag-dos, hen nights and those who just wanted to experience a cheap cruise. Of course there were people who fancied a nice trip to Amsterdam or Hamburg; although, they were few and far between. Many ended up completely swept up in the party culture and rather than be able to beat them they joined them (face down on the disco dance floor). The party cruise (for the crew on ships that have an average guest age of seventy) is something to look forward to. Suddenly the DJ has something to do. The disco dance floor is filled and that isn't with people doing the jive or ballroom dancing. The Officers usually venture out and struggle doing their duties for a few days as they break the rules and have a glass of wine. Just so you know the Officers and crew are randomly breathalysed because there is a no drinking rule on board. If any individual measures more 0.05 they can be dismissed instantly. What makes this more interesting is that the crew and Officers can be off duty and will still be breathalysed. So imagine the temptation for the crew for younger people, partying and the dreaded alcohol temptation. The combinations is a potential cruisey disaster. The crew party into the night and have to still deliver service every day, while the guests roll out of bed when they fancy and begin the cycle of general carnage, hangover-dom and dehydration. As a result, they often go for the hair of the dog solution and neck a beer, a gin or whisky when they wake.

What is worse than a hangover and feeling slightly green? Well that is when the ship hits a storm during a hangover. It is quite a sight watching people determinedly partying when the party platform is pitching and rolling in all directions. The disco dance floor is quite a spectacle to behold when the gyrating group all find themselves unintentionally shimmying to the edge of the dance floor on one side of the room. The ship will then shift and they quickly find themselves on the other side of the dance floor without even trying. It is as if magic has taken place. When there has been a lot of alcohol involved then the dancing can result in piles – where a mass jolt runs through the ship and people are swept off their feet simultaneously. It is hard enough to walk in a sozzled straight-line but when the ship is bouncing about any sort of balance or coordination becomes a real challenge. The dance floor can take on the feeling of an obstacle course while people determinedly shake their stuff while they get shaken.

On an additional note, there are sometimes 'Party Cruisers' who stumble onto the wrong cruise. Somehow something went wrong and the party cruise animals find themselves on a cruise where the average age is seventy-five. With this in mind, this becomes the best kind of spotting potential because you will notice that the party animals can't dampen down so they will do their best to get those of the matured life experience to join in. If you can't beat them then try and get them involved! There have been some magical moments in the disco where a request for something lively has been played and the party animals give it some welly while the older majority cover their ears with their hands and look horrified. Beauty!

## CHAPTER 26

## THE MARRIED OFFICER WITH NUMEROUS WIVES

This little cruisey creaturey delight is a joy to spot, especially if you are gossipy by nature. One has to be really switched on to catch glimpses of this one, or figure out the behind the scenes antics and that is what makes this creature sooooo exciting. One has to pay more attention to body language and space between members of the opposite sexes, and same sexes in many cases. When a crew member arrives on board they are advised 'What goes on a ship stays on the ship,'– oh no it doesn't! How deluded! Ships are a hive of gossip and speculation. When ships spend five or more days at sea then the behind the scenes gossip escalates to a whole new level. At the same time when the 'Launderette Gossips' get their gossipy gobs-a-smacking grips on something that might have potential then speculation travels like engine fire. If a 'Launderette Gossip' senses a liaison, then everyone will soon know, even if it isn't true. According to one gossip the Captain had a whole harem.

To provide a bit of an insight, most Officers spend eight months a year on the ship and four months on land. The crew members are usually between eight and ten months on board at a time, so imagine how challenging that is to maintain a relationship on board or on land, especially when you can be trans-shipped at the drop of a Captain's hat. It seems that many on board lead double lives and that also means double wives or husbands. Wives on land and then a ship wife on board, and sometimes a number of girlfriends, and possibly a boyfriend for good measure. It is rarer for the women to have multiple relationships, I will leave you to figure out why that is, although it does happen. Imagine a husband visiting the ship to meet the wife's new girlfriend. That was quite an interesting event. Of course it is strange how accepted this multiple partner scenario is; however, sometimes people get greedy and there is a wife or husband on land, one on board, a 'fun times' in numerous ports and then there are the liaisons with guests as well (which is not allowed). I still don't get why when those greedy sorts have every porthole filled that they still go ashore and explore the brothels. What makes the situation all the more challenging is when land wifey arrives on board and the ship wifey is on board and everyone knows. In some cases, the land wife accepts the circumstances and enjoys the freedom of their life on land and purely enjoys the limited time on board with their partner. Of course there are times when wives/partners are completely oblivious and a series of events results in an on board discovery. Awkward? Ohhhhh so awkward and quite often a huge spectacle, especially when the discovery takes place at sea and neither partner can make an escape unless they hijack a lifeboat.

One of the more bizarre discoveries was when a ship wife arrived on board. She had a last minute chance to sail with her husband and took it. When she arrived, her Officer husband left her to sleep off her jet lag in his cabin and forgot to advise his 'on board wife'. The on board wife had a key to the cabin and in her break thought she would have a 'nap'. Or as some might say an afternoon of rumpy pumpy which makes it more exciting when the sea is lumpy. A bit of lumpy rumpy pumpy stops you being grumpy – apparently. When the ship wife arrived in the cabin, she assumed that her man was in the bed waiting for her and decided to strip off and join him. Unfortunately for her it wasn't him. Imagine the land wife's shock while being in a half-asleep state and waking up to meet your husband's other woman in her naked state! Picture the surprise for both parties when the ship wife and the on board wife found themselves in bed with each other! Some Officer's dream! As you can envision there was quite a lot of hoooo haaaaa about it all. In addition, there was quite a lot of screaming. Such incidents navigate the ship in a gossipy second but essentially such stories are simply 'ship's shagging' in the night.

## CHAPTER 27

## THE MOBILITY SCOOTER REBELS

Yes I know they have been mentioned in the previous section but these rebels need a bit more attention. There are general scooter antics and then there are those who are more rebellious. It is worth watching out for these naughty sorts because they are quite exciting.

On this particular occasion I had never seen so many people on mobility scooters in one place. It seemed that the cruise ship was adapted for holidaymakers who had menacing motors. You might think that maybe I am being a little bit cruel but oh no. When you have seen two mobility scooter menaces playing chicken with each other to get off a gangway then you will realise that 'Mobility Scooter Rebels' are in fact a dangerous breed of 'Cruise Ship Creature'.

There are times when you witness some of the strangest sights on the ship. Take for example a mobility scooter driver with a learner sign on the back and Barbie hooter and streamers on the front. To make the souped-up motor weirder there was a huge gold horn that made a loud foghorn noise. I first witnessed this creature attempting to reverse out of a lift. Just to provide a scootery insight: most scooters go in forwards and reverse out. She was banging the doors and going back and forth attempting to find her alignment. This is often where the greatest challenge lies with scooter manoeuvres. At one point she revved the engine flew backwards out of the lift at speed. She backed towards a group of unsuspecting lift users. The group scattered and she did what appeared to be a handbrake turn, which rotated the scooter in the direction of the deck, where she accelerated to the door and slammed on her brakes. I was amazed that she wasn't hurt. That wasn't the last time I saw such scooteresque antics either. Further into the cruise the mobility menace befriended two other old dears on scooters. All had long white hair and a rebellious twinkle in their eyes. They became known as the witches of Scooterwick. The two scooteresque gang members had floral basket displays and would often transport half of the buffet around with them. They would zoom past, slam on their brakes and weave amongst the other guests sounding the foghorn. When it was misty on deck they would appear from the fog sounding their foghorns and cackling hysterically. Amongst the fog, screams and revving could be heard as the dangerous driving ensued. In the end the Captain had to caution her and her scooter-witchy-mates. He threatened to remove her learner sign and confiscate her vehicle. She wasn't the only example of such mobility menaces. I have seen a number of people drunk and in charge of a mobility scooter. Where most drunks can't walk in a straight line, this lot can't make it along a corridor without rebounding off walls or colliding with sculptures and floral arrangements.

In addition to the above, there are always the extreme mobility adventurers. You would have thought that the German army had been involved in adapting the mobility scooter of Indiana Mobility Jones. On that particular occasion the mobility scooter appeared to be an all-terrain vehicle that may even travel in water. The all-terrain creation was amazing because the chap could be seen navigating the most extreme environments on a mobility scooter. I half expected him to be seen scaling a vertical cliff face or even the side of a ship. His attitude was that he might not be able to walk but he certainly intended to experience everything, no matter what the terrain was. My only concern was that he would be four-wheel mobility driving over sand dunes in Dubai and his battery would go flat. Help!

You can now understand why the 'Mobility Scooter Rebels' also fall into the more exciting 'Cruise Ship Creature' breed, although of course they could straddle the rebellious and the dangerous breeds too. In fact this creature is so abundant and adaptable that it is certainly worth considering what the more dominant versions of the creature are.

# CHAPTER 28

## THE MISSING IN SWIMWEAR ACTION

This 'Cruise Ship Creature' will capture your attention when you least expect it. You may well find yourself doing a double take as your unconscious figures out what has taken place. Is that person nude on deck? Nope. It seems that their swimwear is either beige, very small or white and wet resulting in transparency. Sometimes the more portly passengers unintentionally cover their trunks or bikinis with excess flesh. Others have that unfortunate moment where they have selected an item that looks good in the shop but haven't considered the consequences of applying water to the item which turns it see-through. This scenario is the 'King's New Clothes' of swimwear. When you can technically see what someone had for breakfast (chipolatas and a couple of boiled eggs or bacon, a bean and fried onions) and no one has the courtesy to point out that you can see the details of the said 'breakfasty undercarriage'. Of course no one wants to be the one who advises that details can be seen, although one of my more brash friends advised one of my colleagues that his swim shorts were so see-through that she could see detail. He found it funny until she said, 'I notice you have been circumcised too.' That was when he realised that his white swimming shorts were somewhat revealing.

In addition to the above is when the swimwear unintentionally evacuates through pressure, wind or not fitting. On some ships there are waterslides and wave pools. These are prime locations for tied bikinis to depart for the other end of the pool, or wedgy into complete disappearance. In some cases strings get caught and result in swimwear stranding or suspension. There is nothing worse than catching a bikini bottom on a door handle, to continue unaware and have the whole bikini bottom disentangle itself from one's body and remain attached to the door. You may just hope the tan lines create a decent decoy.

Another fabulous moment involved a swim with dolphins' tour. As part of the tour the guests were able to swim with dolphins and could be propelled across the pool by a lovely dolphin. This took place at a large open pool that had a beautifully large underwater window so that groups could watch dolphins swimming while the tourists were launched through the water.

During this particular tour a group of school children entered the aquarium. At the same moment a guest was lined up to be guided at high speed across the pool. With the sudden swimming surge the guest screamed excitedly (or so everyone thought) as she zoomed across the pool pushed by the dolphin. Actually what the shrill scream was - was the moment where she realised her bikini bottoms left her person and remained on the other side of the pool. Obviously the school group had an insight into female biology that they had not expected that day.

## PART 3

## THE QUIRKY CRUISE SHIP CREATURES

Quite often the word quirky is used to describe weirdness politely. This section contains 'Cruise Ship Creatures' that can make you wonder about life, humanity and the state of the universe. They are fun to observe, will inspire you to ask yourself existential questions and provide an insight into how a cruise ship can influence people to do things that they would not consider doing on land.

## CHAPTER 29

### THE 'CAPTAIN'S HAT WEARERS'

I never really understood what it was that made a person decide that it was a good idea to adorn a Captain's hat the moment they arrived at the cruise terminal. First of all that person is clearly not the Captain because they are not wearing a uniform, and what is it they are actually trying to say? 'Don't worry if the ship sinks because I have a Captain's hat!' Are they saying 'I have been a Captain?' Do they wear it as some kind of talking point? 'Oh lovely Captain's hat you have there,' has said no one ever! So with all that in mind, I have spent many years travelling on ships and watching the Captain's Hat brigade. No matter how hard I try I just can't figure out what the appeal is. There have been numerous times where I have been tempted to ask, yet it does seem rude – 'Why do you wear a Captain's hat when you are not a Captain, have never been a Captain and unless you intend to create a mutiny why would you wear it?' Ahhh I think I just figured it out... They wear the Captain's hat to suggest they could be mutiny leaders. Hmmm I just wouldn't follow someone because they happened to be wearing a Captain's hat. Would you? In all honesty I think I could be haunted by people wearing Captain's hats. Thank goodness they don't carry stuffed Captain's cats around with them too because that would be just too weird. Quirky? Erm yes!

# CHAPTER 30

## THE 'WE JUST LOVE TO DANCE'

Some people just love to dance. They might clearly like to show people how much they love to dance. When a person has a passion then why not share it? The 'We Just Love To Dance' creature will take every opportunity to show their moves whether it is at a sail away, to a live band or in the dance classes. Sometimes they don't even need music or can be carried along by the music in their headphones. They dance away like they are attending a silent disco. Some love dancing so much that they take the opportunity to tap dance along the deck, especially when practising for the talent show. There were complaints from a cabin when a group of ten rather portly ladies took to the decks to practice their tap dancing routine before the talent show. 'It sounds like elephants stampeding in high heels,' said the complainer.

Other 'We Just Love To Dance' creatures behave as though they are the stars of Dirty Dancing and you can find them practising in the strangest areas like in the library or in front of the ship's napper. Some practice dancey lifts in the pool but that is a Dirty Dancing cliché! If there is a secret nook there may well be someone doing a shimmy because they quite simply love to dance. Imagine the lift/elevator opening to reveal someone dancing to the music inside. Good on them, they just love to dance!

There are of course dance lessons and on some ships there are gentleman hosts allocated to the role of dance host. That is where the dancing can become rather exciting. According to the gentleman hosting rules there shouldn't be any special attention given to any particular guests. There have been ladies who time the dance hosts and will cut in or tap their watch at the end of a dance. Who would have thought that the love of dancing could create some juicy conflict?

If you ever want a bit of solid entertainment, then attend any of the dance classes on board. You can learn to tap dance, salsa or ballroom dance. The details will be listed in the ship's paper and to say that it is fun would be an understatement. Sometimes there is an air of competition and haughty dancing superiority but that in itself is amusing especially if the 'Phantom Blow Off' (you will find out more about this character later) is in the room. Of course there will be some fantastic dancers who are there to show their natural ability. Alternatively, if you have the coordination of a drunken giraffe climbing onto a hammock then it is precisely the opportunity to challenge yourself and demonstrate moves never witnessed before in public. No one said you have to be good at dance to just love to dance!

# CHAPTER 31

## THE SHIP LOVERS

Ships are a real passion to some guests. They like to stroke the bannisters, sniff all the flowers and then spend hours admiring the ship's map. Where there are large pictures of the ship they can be found gazing lovingly at their object of shippy affection. 'Ship Lovers' spend an uncanny amount of time studying the Officer and crew photographs, especially when the ship is at sea. You often walk past and they are in deep discussion about the career of certain individuals and whether they have met them on other ships. The 'Ship Lovers' adore knowing everything about the ship. They have been on numerous galley tours, taken the back of house tour, where they get to see the ship's innards and can share pictures of the different refurbishments. They have peered into crew cabins and sit in the front row for the Captain's question time. They love the ship, love sailing on the ship and every time they step on the gangway they fall in love again. This 'Cruise Ship Creature' is fascinating because they love to share their passion and will undoubtedly have insights that you would not discover unless you set up an interrogation room for the crew.

# CHAPTER 32

## THE INSANE AND THE ECCENTRIC

The shippy 'Eccentric' creatures are often quite amusing. There was one wonderful guest who piled her hair high with multi-coloured chopsticks to make a nest. She then arranged fake birds in the creation. She wore round red-rimmed glasses, red lipstick and a huge grin. She was also rather partial to wearing black and white striped tights. Whenever I saw her I smiled because of her attire. Formal nights were fantastic because that nest of hair was back-combed and planets, suns and moons with dangling asteroids adorned the matted creation. It was as if the universe was re-creating itself in hair-form and her attire matched with a big-bang sparkle.

At the other end of the scale was the Captain's hat and the budgie smuggler saga. This time it was a man with a rather small pair of budgie smugglers that would parade around the pool wearing a Captain's hat. It was amusing at first until he started wearing the full Captain's outfit and was found wandering around the crew area. Obviously he had to be escorted out but back to the 'Don't you know who I am?' syndrome. Well he pulled that one out the bag 'You can call me Captain.' That takes me onto the next batch of randomers: the 'Completely Insane'.

Anyone can book a cruise and there is no limit on how nuts a person can be. There is no psychometric testing or referencing before guests arrive on a ship. In some cases, going on a cruise ship is the opportunity to reveal their extreme levels of loopiness. The 'Completely Insane' blend in at first but there are clues. The first is that whatever they say makes no sense. At first you might forgive them for being a bit daft. After a little while there is a certain feeling of discomfort and you might wonder whether there is an element of compulsive lying. It is once you have been lulled into a false sense of security that you realise. While I was in the Caribbean I climbed onto a catamaran with some guests. One of them summoned me over, as though I was her servant, and said 'Do you have the after sun?' My response was no. 'Why would I carry after sun on a tour with me when I hadn't even been in the sun? Surely we would have to be in the sun first.' She then went round the boat and asked everyone. After a while she became somewhat obsessed by the fact that no one carried after sun. She stood up and screamed 'How am I supposed to get sun burnt if there is no after sun? Didn't any of you consider that?' Quite clearly no one considered the fact a stranger might need after sun to get sunburned. This lady developed somewhat of a reputation on the ship for weird requests. She wanted to take her lobster out on the deck so it could see the sea for the last time before she ate it. Clearly the lobster was already dead. What do you do with that? They have paid for a holiday and they have to be looked after like everyone else. There have been times when people have arrived on the ship and had full meltdowns. It is as if they have finally found a place to rest and all their pent-up tension and issues unfold. There was a chap who would spend a lot of the day in the lift. When anyone entered he would press every single button for each floor. When he was questioned about what he was doing, he replied 'I have to press them all otherwise we will all die.' I think most people departed the lift at the next floor and used the stairs.

# CHAPTER 33

## THE GYM FUNNIES

There are gym goers, gym bunnies and then there are a rare type of gym attendee known as the 'Gym Funnies'. Cruise ships seem to gather a variety of these characters. The first hint of this type of cruisey creature is when you notice a chap with knee-high yellow socks and brown sandals jogging on the treadmill wearing his adventure outfit. In his own mind he is an adventurer or some intrepid treadmill explorer but in reality he simply is a conundrum. I still haven't figured out how these 'Gym Funnies' get away with it. However, that then leads me into the next 'Gym Funny' type. On many cruise ships the average age is seventy and above. Many wear hearing aids, which is quite normal; however, wearing hearing aids and huge earphones is quite a bizarre combination especially when they burst into song. Oh yes I almost fell off the rowing machine when the chap beside me, wearing his earphones, began singing at the top of his lungs as if no one could hear him. When I glanced across at him, you might have thought that he would stop. Nope, in fact he just sang louder. I finished my allocated training time and moved across the room. I chose a machine where I could observe. Was the man a nutter or was he purposely bursting into song next to unsuspecting guests? There are people who do that kind of thing for entertainment and to gauge reactions. Well it seemed that the chap was suffering from Oblivionosis. This is an invented syndrome (I invented it) where the person is so oblivious and unaware of others that he or she believes his behaviour is normal and non-offensive. Well he did offend me, so I continued to watch. Unfortunately he was aggravating the other guests too. Some of them were so outburst shocked, rather than say something, they just moved away. They were polite like me. Well when it came to the end of my workout we did cross paths. The burning question on my lips was are you singing loudly on purpose? So I asked him... Guess what? He had no idea at all that he was singing. He said that he got so into his workout that he didn't think about anything else. He said there were even times that he almost forgot where he was. That made me think there was more to the singer than being a 'Gym Funny'.

One of the most awkward situations with a 'Gym Funny' was when a lady in her eighties turned up for an exercise class wearing a gold lame leotard. That in itself is a little awkward; however, the instructor went with it and didn't make any comment. Anyway as the group stretched they all opened their legs. It seemed the leotard was buttoned around the undercarriage (lady garden) and with one motion all the buttons popped. With a loud ping, the little old dear's leotard transformed into more of a boob tube. Yes, unfortunate. Unfortunately the instructor was sitting with her back to multiple mirrors and this lady was at the front of the exercise class. Unfortunately, a multitude of growlers reflected back at the class. As always people were polite and continued their stretches while the instructor mentioned the issue to the old lady. It seemed that she thought that it had become a bit 'airy and free' in the area below. She managed to sort herself out and the instructor gave her a pair of shorts to cover her credentials so she could finish the class. So rather than the 'Gym Funny' maybe that little episode should be renamed the 'Gym Growler'.

Talking of growling, that leads perfectly onto the final example of 'Gym Funnies' and that is the 'Gym Grunter'. It really is amazing the level of grunt that can be achieved from someone lifting weights. What makes it increasingly exciting is when the ship is rocking. The grunting noises seem to be combined with guttural retching. I am going to deviate for a moment. I am always fascinated by how dedicated people are who attend the gym; however, there is a breed of gym goers who will still attend the gym in the hugest storms. The fact that running on a treadmill when the ship is rising and falling becomes dangerous won't stop them. Numerous guests still attempt a full workout despite the conditions, okay I may well be one of those people... Yep the feeling of running up a hill one moment and then speeding down a hill the next, without changing treadmill gradients may well be the appeal. Essentially running on a treadmill while the ship is in a storm is stupidity at its best. It is a very real problem and people do get thrown off, so the spa staff actually have to disconnect those machines or even close the gym to stop people being catapulted across the room. If guests have the opportunity to use the machines then they will.

Now, back to the grunters... So I have noticed that the speed and pitch of grunt depends on the size of swell and motion direction. On a calm sea day the grunts can be likened to a medium size grunt. If you think medium sized pig on a farm kind of grunt. As the waves increase the grunts begin to surpass themselves. There are mating walrus imitations and the extreme grunt that comes from two randy elephants reaching a climax. The general grunter is male, it isn't often you hear a woman properly grunt in the gym; however, there are the female equivalents which I call the 'Orgasmics' where they make noises as though satisfied in a sausage-penetration sense. They increase their exercise and their pleasurable noise response escalates. I have witnessed this mainly in yoga but there are a few who gain 'pleasure' from gym escapades. One woman bent over and increased her breathing so much so that she became lost in her bend and reached a state that only could be described as ecstatic. In the commotion two chaps flew backwards off their treadmills and a number of dumbbells tumbled to the floor.  When she composed herself and stood up, it was as if the room had been annihilated by a fanny-tastic whirlwind. She strutted with a flush and a hippy motion to the female changing room. Obviously that workout made her feel particularly good and inspired men in a way that their grunts became increasingly manly!

# CHAPTER 34

## THE ALWAYS LOST

Isn't it amazing that even on that last day of a cruise, after guests have been travelling on a ship for three weeks, passengers still need to ask how to get off the ship? Quite astounding really! During disembarkation guests would ask, 'So how do I get off the ship?' Just so you know, there were plenty of signs and arrows pointing to the gangway. I would be polite and direct them and then there would always be that comment: 'You would have thought that we would know that by now.' There were a number of potential replies, however, a polite smile with a nod would always suffice (rather than kick them up the bottom and call them an idiot!) Tolerance levels do wear thin and every cruise repeating the same pattern can be a challenge especially at the end of a contract. Guests who have travelled for only four days could be forgiven, yet guests who took the world cruise could not. World cruise guests on average have usually sailed on the ship for over one hundred nights, so when they ask you how to get off the ship or where so and so is... then you wonder whether they actually don't know or whether they are taking their last opportunity to have someone think for them. I would believe it is the latter. Service until the end and get your money's worth may well be the motto.

So not only do people have a challenge leaving the ship at the end of the cruise, it is always fascinating watching people trying to figure out where everything is on the first day. You see people making sudden turns in the corridor and many realising they are the wrong deck. That is normal; however, there are those who are 'Always Lost'. They step out of the lift, stride in one direction, stop and realise that they don't actually know where they are. What makes navigation challenging is when you are in the centre of the ship because it is difficult to figure out which direction is forward and aft. Of course if you walk in one direction for a while you will arrive somewhere. You then have the opportunity to step out on deck to see which way the ship is sailing and use that to navigate where you want to go. It appears there are quite a few passengers who have not figured that out yet and that may well be why they spend their time 'Always Lost'.

There are times when you are walking through the crew area, which looks like a white metallic hospital, and a guest happens to have taken a wrong door into the metal labyrinth. So not only are they lost, they have now wandered into a whole new shippy universe. If being lost wasn't enough, they have emerged into an entirely alien new world and quite often they then manage to lose themselves in that too. When you find guests wandering around crew cabins with a concerned facial expression of confusion and frustration, you know you have discovered an 'Always Lost' in a state of evolution... They go from 'Always Lost' to 'Completely and Extremely Lost!'

# CHAPTER 35

## THE INTREPID EXPLORERS

You might be amazed that some people think that they are 'Intrepid Cruise Explorers'. Some may dress like they are about to traverse the Antarctic and they are just going to Belgium. Of course there are those that dress as though they are going to find lost cities in the Amazon when they are simply going to the Mediterranean. These creatures are visually obvious because many have Explorer hats or Pith helmets. Some will carry mosquito nets, wear khaki-colour clothing or even better a nice bit of camouflage. What makes camouflage particularly exciting is that it stands out on a ship. Unless someone wears all white and body paints their face and hair to blend in, then they will generally stand out against the crisp white background. That is unless they choose to lurk amongst the fake foliage dotted about the ship. Anyway enough of chameleon-esque solutionising for ships.

Anyway I deviated, when it comes to cruises that go to South America, Africa or the Middle East, that is when the 'Intrepid Explorer' creature comes into its own. Embarkation day is filled with Explorer hats, Pith helmets and Corked hats. It seems that the embarking passengers have recently watched Indiana Jones or Tarzan. There are no leather whips allowed on board, so they are confiscated from luggage during the mandatory security scans. There could be a room on board filled with whips, and not for a Fifty Shades of Grey reunion.

When it comes to safari tours you will watch the 'Intrepid Explorer' creatures gather by four wheel drives. They will spray themselves with all manner of mosquito repellent, pile on the sun cream and out khaki each other. There are often special vests with far too many pockets to accommodate every potential survival and photographic wear. I do find this cruisy breed fascinating because you can understand them gathering in their 'Intrepid Explorer' way; however, sometimes they do take it a little too far and stride about ports in that same intrepid wear. Of course it is funny but wholly inappropriate in places such as the Greek Islands or New York. I guess it is a case of once an explorer - always an explorer.

# CHAPTER 36

## THE 'WE ARE SO ACTIVE'

Quick touch your toes as people pass or do a stretch when other guests least expect it. This couple, and it is usually a couple, who are sooooo active that you are amazed they have time for anything else. They are easy to spot because they quite often wear matching outfits (of the tracksuit kind) or they wear those ultra-flappy running shorts. This pair are so active that they don't seem to rest and look at other guests in horror when they are relaxing, especially on sun loungers. The expression on their faces is curious and might suggest they are asking the question: 'Why would you want to do nothing when you can be in constant motion?'

This couple are often up and out on the deck at 5.30am, they run the deck, stroll the deck, stretch on the deck and then run some more. They eat their lunch and within the hour they are circumnavigating the decks with that extreme bottom-wiggling walk. The pendulous swinging bottoms synch up into a mesmerising rhythm as the pair pound the decks with a marching stomp. Their eyes are glazed as they demonstrate how active two people can be. Once the pair have destroyed the decks they then move into the gym. I have witnessed tandem step ups and kettle bell swinging. Shortly after they can be found rolling around the floor looking like they are humping the foam rollers. The foam rollers smooth their knotted muscles and give them the perfect opportunity to roll back and forth to the ship's motion. Still it does look like they are humping the floor.

Later in the evening there will be a formal night or some kind of dancing and guess who is dominating the dance floor? Yep the 'We Are So Actives' are demonstrating the can-can, the jive and the salsa – all at once. I have often wondered whether these type are actually caffeine addicts or have been consuming something stronger. At the end of the evening I would half expect them to do a Dirty Dancing lift before making their way to bed. That pair continue the same regime day after day, they might mix it up with a bit of swimming and become the 'Swimming Pool Hoggers'. Yet is it really a holiday when you are so active? What about rest, recuperation and general gluttony? Of course, we all have different ideas about the ideal holiday. The 'We Are So Active' encourage other guests to eat on their behalf because surely there has to be a law of physics where when people are so active they burn calories on behalf of the face-stuffers.

# CHAPTER 37

## THE MAP SALIVATORS

Have you ever watched a man gaze deliriously as though he is in love? Strangely it is usually men who reveal such an expression on ships as they gaze at the wall. It is the same expression that turns up on their face when they see a top of the range sports car, a new and exclusive gadget or super deluxe yacht. It is a dreamy face combined with desire and a hint of salivation. Now can you imagine this response from someone when they gaze longingly at a map? Well it happens on the ship, it might also happen in museums too but it isn't often one witnesses a display of map-loving-affection in public. It is worth keeping your eyes peeled for this little beauty. Some 'Map Salivators' literally line up waiting for the new navigational maps showing the ship's course. They fidget with excitement when the Bridge Officer places the navigational piece of art in the ship's navigation cabinet. They are like dedicated train spotters and wait with great anticipation when the next leg of the cruise journey is revealed in mappy form. What provides the greatest excitement is the positioning of the small golden ship on the drawn-out route for the coming days. I read somewhere, a long time ago, that for men maps are like gazing upon a naked woman's body. Who knows? Men and women are very different and I am a woman. I guess maps reveal lumps, bumps and patches of water. I don't quite understand how that correlates to gazing at a woman's body... Hang on... Maybe it does. I think that is for you to work out yourself.

The 'Map Salivators' can usually be found anywhere there is a map on display or to be displayed. Now the ultimate dream for these creatures is a visit to the bridge. On the bridge the Navigational Officer can be overwhelmed by questions by the mappacious-loving creatures. Unfortunately, the Navigational Officer has to cope with strange delirious expressions as the map perverts desperately want to grope at previous maps, rare maps or maps that show large expanses of sea with all the depths listed along with the troughs.

There have been times when there have been heated debates within the 'Map Salivator' ranks about the best courses to take, and intense questioning as to why certain routes were selected. When the bridge visit comes to the end, trying to get the mappy sorts to leave is a challenge. The levels of resistance and the increase in questioning to buy time is quite apparent. If they had their way, then they would spend most of their cruise up on the bridge making suggestions on navigation.

To intensify this particular 'Cruise Ship Creature' spotting you may like to observe the following: when people have a passion they often desire to share it. It is very sweet watching the map lovers attempt to share their absolute love of maps with their spouses or partners. Where the 'Map Salivators' have a look of longing, their partners have a look of complete boredom as they do their best to understand their partner's desire. Admittedly some people have their obsessions and when 'Map Salivators' unite in the map-loving lust there is a spiral of enthusiasm among them. When they examine the islands on route and look at the depths of the ocean they are traversing you can sense their delight. It is quite lovely to witness and that is why this creature is rather nice to watch. They could make it easier for you to identify them and all they need to acquire is a brown Mackintosh. That would mean that they may well join the ranks of trainspotters and flashers.

CHAPTER 38

## THE 'I CAN'T HEAR YOU DARLING. WHAT DID YOU SAY?'

There are some rather amusing situations that develop when the average guest age on a ship is seventy. What is amazing is how the upper age range can reach ninety-nine. In this one instance it was fascinating to listen to a group of people who all professed to mishear, not particularly hear and certainly not pay attention. I first met the older group at an Officer's table where they advised me that a number of them were challenged in the hearing realm and could quite often go off on some quite remarkable tangents. Take for example one of them fancied a burger the other told him off for swearing. 'Darling saying oh bugger at the dinner table is hardly appropriate.'

'Oh,' said another, 'I thought he was going to tell us a story about a burglar.'

'No not a burglar- a burger. I wouldn't want to eat a burglar now would I? Nor would I bugger one if you will excuse the French. Burger buggery is equally odd if you ask me.'

That was the opening conversation. How do you respond to that?

'Mayonnaise anyone?'

What became increasingly curious was how the mishearing stories developed into their own fascinating tales. After a few wines the conversation became all the more challenging with loud slurs and less capacity to concentrate. Obviously the volume increased and the whole dining room was unintentionally involved in the conversation.

'Soooo Dianne here went on a twelve-week suppository class. It was amazing how she utilised leather and brocade,' said one of the gentlemen.

Around the table were varying nods as each came up with their own individual stories.

'Surely there is only a limited amount of ways that one can administer a suppository. How do they make it last twelve weeks?' said one of the others.

'Oh my dear you need to be more creative.'

There were frowns and slightly squinty faces as the group imagined the various scenarios.

'Each week you are given a brief and you can be as creative as you like...'

Admittedly I had heard the word suppository too, so was caught up within the creative imagining challenge of how creative you could be with such an item.

'One week we were focused on metal and another wood,' Dianne announced with a sense of glee.

By this point I felt it wasn't fair for me to ask any questions; instead the expression of completely bemused graced my face.

'In fact we have used the course to re-decorate the lounge.' Gerald announced.

Were there suppository mobiles or maybe art photographs of the little blighters? How do you redecorate a lounge with something that essentially was shoved up someone's anus? Life astounds me!

'The armchair looks so vibrant now.'

I glanced around the table to see whether I was the only one at a complete loss as to why the armchair might be happier after a suppository course.

'Darlings can we just check what that twelve-week course actually was because I sense we may have all misheard.'

'Upholstery... Why what did you think I said?'

There were coughs and laughs from around the table. 'Ahhhh upholstery. We did wonder how you could make a twelve-week course from suppositories.'

There was chuckling and chortling from all around the table. There might have been even a loud guffaw.


'Oh that reminds us of the Vagina incident,' said one of the other guests at the table.

'We were talking about naming the new ship in the fleet and someone rudely shouted out that we should rename her Regina, this was misheard by the entire Captain's Welcome Aboard Party as Vagina. No one wanted to call them on it until an old lady said, 'I think that is a marvellous name. It has a real ring to it. I love it!' She clapped with delight.

The Captain was silent for a while and the room was awkward as everyone tried to figure out what they had heard, and what she had heard.

The old lady, from her wheelchair beamed, 'Regina what a wonderful name for a ship – so elegant and regal.' There was laughing around the room.

'Well I rather liked the idea of a vagina sailing across the Atlantic,' said a defiant older man with a Father Christmas beard. 'Oh Terrence,' said his wife in a tone of dismay.

The Captain took a deep breath, 'Yes Regina has a certain ring to it; however, we are looking for something a little more modern.'

'A fresh vagina!' replied the defiant old man.

'How terribly rude,' said the Captain in his most dignified tone. 'Something elegant and graceful.'

'A graceful vagina!' replied the old chap finding himself ever-so amusing.

'I think we should change the subject now sir!' The Captain used a certain tone, which made it very clear that the conversation would not continue.


When it came to desert, Gerald asked for a slurred 'Ice cream – yes a nice bit of chocolate' and Terrence responded 'Haemorrhoids are blighters aren't they?'

The table tended to agree as they filtered through what Terrence had heard. Later I learned that 'Arse cream' was what had been heard.

The table of guests laughed at the incident and it certainly made an impression – maybe one that was best forgotten. The next day I escorted a tour where a wife-of-the-mishearing-kind interpreted stories that a guide was sharing with the bus. It was then that I realised that an entire history could be completely re-created through the act of mishearing. So with regards to 'Cruise Ship Creatures' – this group are quite a fascinating group because there are Chinese whisperers, there are gossips and there is a mishearing faction who could unintentionally change the course of history.

# CHAPTER 39

## THE CRAFTY CRAFTERS

I often wonder how people manage to smuggle knitting needles onto a cruise ship when everything is put through a security scanner. The thing is, there are people who are dedicated to crafting. I have witnessed felt making, watercolour painting, batik, tapestry and there are numerous kinds of knitters. One of the most amusing things is how often the knitters sit in the front row of the theatres for shows or for the lectures and knit. Yep, a professional lecturer is delivering the talk of their life and there is someone bloody knitting while they talk. Alternatively, there is a highly energetic dance show and there is a knitter yawning and creating a three armed sweater. Love it.

# CHAPTER 40

## THE 'HAS ANYONE HANDED IN MY TEETH?'

The 'Has Anyone Handed In My Teeth?' is a very rare type of passenger. I had to add them to the 'Cruise Ship Creatures' because quite frankly there are days on the ship where bemusement evolves into the question of 'How has humanity survived this long?' So this rather sweet lady, who was nearing five foot on tip toes and resembled a white haired sack, asked whether her teeth had been handed in. This made the question, how would we know they were her teeth? Were teeth often handed in? Was there an entire box filled with dental creations with people's names on them? If people were handing in other people's teeth then what other weird and wonderful items lurked in the lost and found box?

So the gummy little lady was asked when she last had her teeth and she could not remember. It was only when she went to dinner that evening that she realised that she had forgotten them. So guess what happened next? Housekeeping (all the room stewards) were advised to search their areas for a set of teeth. After about half an hour there was no response and the little old lady realised it was likely that she was going to have to live on liquidised food for the rest of her cruise. It was all very sad until the beautiful moment when one of the cabin stewards dashed up to the reception desk wielding a set of teeth. 'They were in the base of a plant pot by the café,' he said. How the teeth ended up in the plant pot is a mystery in itself. The old lady studied the teeth. 'No they're not them.' She didn't even try them for size. With a dejected look she toddled off and paused. She lifted her hand in the air and waved a set of teeth. 'Found them,' they were in the inside pocket of my bag under a tissue. Silly me.'

A set of gnashers sat with some spinach wedged between the two front teeth on the reception desk. For a while no one said anything. It was just one of those curious moments where you wonder what kind of divine entity had such humour. How long had those teeth been sitting in a plant pot? Who was without their teeth and had not realised? Did false teeth grow on trees?

## PART 4

## THE RARE CRUISE SHIP CREATURE BREEDS

The below are rare breeds of 'Cruise Ship Creatures' because they don't draw attention to themselves and are often relatively stealthy. Have you noticed that when people are happy they don't generally draw attention to themselves? It seems that people are drawn to negativity and drama. The way I see it is if you shine a torch on a turd then you get an illuminated turd. Yes – I know I have mentioned this before! The shimmering shit basically distracts you from seeing the nice things going on. So when it comes to shining your torch on something then why not search out the nice things, nice people and happy times? With this in mind, enjoy this section and it is worth searching these cruisey creatures out. The more you see them then the naughtier and nastier 'Cruise Ship Creatures' will disappear from the cruising periphery.

# CHAPTER 41

## THE LOVELY ONES

There are many 'Cruise Ship Creatures' to behold and many that may well seem a little weird and those who you want to avoid; however, there are some really lovely 'Cruise Ship Creatures'. There are guests who love every moment of their voyage. They smile and say hello and mean it. When they ask how you are, they fancy a fun conversation. They aren't trying to lure you in so they can complain. Those wonderful 'Cruise Ship Creatures' interact with the other guests in such a way that they uplift them. There are lovely guests who travel solo and those who travel in couples. They don't go round finding fault; instead, they spend time simply enjoying every glorious moment of their time on board. The 'Lovely Ones' can be seen holding hands strolling about the deck, when they are a couple. The single ones seem to befriend half of the ship in the first few days. They will probably only befriend 'half of the ship' to that limit because they seem to have a natural radar that selectively discounts the moaners and complainers. The 'Lovely Ones' are excited when the ship sails into port. They will be up on deck at sunrise and they will make sure that they enjoy all of the activities they fancy. In fact, the 'Lovely Ones' are just wonderful and their positive aura lifts others and provides the rose-tinted glasses for others to view life through. In all honesty, the world travel phenomenon would be an increasingly wonderful place if all the lovelies got together on one ship and went on a voyage of loveliness. Everything would be lovely... and... everyone would be elevated into a state of bliss. Imagine how nice that would be! Infectious cruising loveliness! Amazing!

# CHAPTER 42

## THE NEWBIES

I like the 'Newbies' because everything is so new and fresh for them. Admittedly they spend the first week completely lost and have no clue where they are at all. You often see them step out of a lift and just stand in silence trying to figure out whether they are on the right floor, at the front or rear of the ship or whether they are on the ship. I have seen 'Newbies' walk in circles endlessly looking for their cabin quite simply because they cannot work out which way the ship is moving so can't work out which is the port or starboard side. For the whole cruise they carry the ship's map and on the final day of disembarkation they still keep getting lost. My favourite moment is watching 'Newbies' trying to find the gangway on the first port of arrival. They follow the signs but usually don't find the way out. Of course being new to the world of cruising, one doesn't want to admit that they don't know. Of course the crew can spot a 'Newbie' at ten paces. They just have the 'Newbie' aura.

# CHAPTER 43

## THE TOO IN LOVE TO NOTICE

A group of old dears could tap dance naked past these two and their loving gaze would not falter. The Phantom Raspberry Blower could raucously raspberry blow between the pair of them and there wouldn't even be a flicker of a response. The ship could rock to the point where people rebound like human pinballs. All the while, these two would maintain direct eye contact, dazed loving expressions and then dive into yet another intensive snog. At first I thought this type of 'Cruise Ship Creature' had experienced hypnosis, were snoggacious cannibals (through extreme snoggerage) or were in some kind of misty daze but no... I was completely wrong - they are clearly in love.

To make it easier to spot them, they will have a table for two in the restaurant. They will literally gaze at each other and smile. Sometimes they don't have to talk because clearly they communicate through non-expressive dance, blinks and general mind reading. How food arrives in their mouths is quite a conundrum. Another hint - the pair have a contented glow about them. A glow fills the atmosphere wherever they sit and you may find blue birds singing classic songs surreptitiously beside them. When Bambi strolls into the restaurant and serenades them, then you have discovered the 'Too In Love To Notice'.

CHAPTER 44

## THE 'THOSE YOU DON'T NOTICE'

Have you ever tried noticing people that don't stand out? It really is quite a random pastime. You would not believe how many people you can notice that you would not normally notice when you put your mind to noticing those who do not stand out. Of course there are many of these people in life and no doubt you may not have noticed them because they are unnoticeable. So the 'Unnoticeables' of this world are a specific kind of creature and could very well work as shippy spies. They could literally be standing next to you but nothing about them makes you go… hang on, there is someone standing next to me, unless they bite your bottom in the buffet queue. Incidentally bottom biting is not a common pastime on ships. It is unusual for a bottom biting bonanza to begin unless an 'Unnoticeable' becomes annoyed when they have filled their tray. Obviously they are carrying that tray with both hands and want to gain the attention of the person in front of them who clearly has no clue they are there. What other alternatives are there in such a situation other than bite that person's bottom?

There are many occasions where 'Unnoticeables' are not noticed. You may well sit in front of them on a bus, or cross-train at the gym beside them but nothing about them draws your attention. When it comes to formal night there is no extreme sparkle or gravity defying hairdos for men or women of the 'Unnoticeable' kind. The 'Unnoticeable' often travel as a couple, they don't join large dining table groups or if they do – they don't really join in. In a crowd they are like chameleons and ashore they evaporate into the crowds. There are times when I wonder whether the 'Unnoticeables' are purposely blending in. That is why I like to retrain my visual filters to notice them and go and talk to them. There is something rather rebellious about noticing that which is not noticeable and it reminds me of the game I-spy combined with Hide-and-seek. Fun can be found on sea days tallying up all the people that you would not normally notice and finding common denominators between them. I will give you a clue – quite often there are beige trousers or shorts involved. Grey seems to be their colour of choice in most clothing.

CHAPTER 45

THE 'WE'RE GETTING MARRIED'

When it comes to getting married you would be surprised how many people choose to cruise into married life. If you think about it, well it is quite logical because you can combine your honeymoon with your marriage ceremony. You then have an excuse to limit the numbers of who come. That may sound cynical but that is a real reason why many people marry on ships: they can be guest selective and only pick people who would enjoy a cruise.

This type of 'Cruise Ship Creature' is easy to spot because one of them usually wears a big white dress. Of course there are gay couples that get married on ships and they can be seen styling out the double groom outfits or a pair of white wedding dresses. What's more, they offer absolute hilarity because there are a lot of 'Ooooh Officer' and 'Ooooh hello Captain' comments throughout the cruise. Of course the Captain maintains his dignity and is aware that the celebrations are likely to descend into extreme-party-carnage.

In the meantime, prior to the marriage the mixed sex couple can be witnessed around the ship gazing at each other very obviously. In some cases, they can't keep their hands off each other and snogging-fests could be likened to gannets feeding their young through regurgitation. There are guests who find the love thing sweet while others retch or make very loud huffs at the spectacle. Other than that the couples need to practise strolling lovingly around the deck in search of the right photographic locations. All in all there is something magical about being married on a ship and many couples who have tied the cruising marriage knot often return years later to renew their vows.

As much as to some it is sickening to witness couples consume each other's face in the name of cruising love, it reminds many of the other couples of that time when they were first married. To some it illuminates them and they are enthused by amorous affection while for others it makes them consider jumping overboard. Whatever way the tide goes there is nothing like a lovely cruisey wedding to bring out the romance in those who have suppressed it.

# CHAPTER 46

## THE ASH SPRINKLERS

This is one of those situations that you couldn't make up and this one is rather bizarre to say the least. Before you read further it is quite dark in terms of situations; however, many people do have ceremonies to sprinkle ashes. Quite often those who have cruised for years, who have really loved their time on ships, ask for their relatives, as their last wish, to sprinkle their ashes from the ship. Many of them provide the funds for the family to experience the most exclusive cruise in absolute luxury so that their ashes can be sprinkled out to sea. On one of these occasions, when I was a photographer, I was asked to photograph an ash sprinkling ceremony.

The Captain made a beautiful speech, the family shared some poems and a eulogy. The group moved to the back of the ship for the release of the ashes and gazed out at the ocean, it was pretty lively at that time. At this point I wondered about divine humour and how dark it can be. The widow opened the canister and began to sprinkle at sunset. It was a beautiful moment to photograph. The ashes were caught on the wind and lifted to the heavens, the rouge radiance of the sun illuminated the ascending ash. The widow emptied the final remnants from the canister. The group gazed up to heaven, there was silence amongst the group and Officers, who wore their tropical whites and looked so dignified. I continued to photograph the ascension which suddenly shifted. The peaceful looking expressions transformed as the wind seized the ashes and blew them back at force at the party and the Officers on deck. A beautiful ascension became a back blast of ash and the group were coated in the deceased's remains. I had already taken the photos on rapid fire before I realised what had taken place. It looked as though an explosion of soot had coated the Officers in their whites. A first the group were silent but then the widow, once she had wiped her face, began to laugh. 'Oh that is so Jerry and his bloody humour!' The full sequence of images were captured and the group purchased them to remember such a strange event. Somewhat bizarre eh?

# CHAPTER 47

## THE DO NOT DISTURB SIGN

Now this 'Do Not Disturb Sign' creature type wasn't on the original list; however, these cruising creatures are more common than I originally thought. It seems that people can be confused by Do Not Disturb signs. One lady phoned reception and said that she had been stuck in her cabin all day. She wanted to know how to get out. The receptionist advised her to go to the door and open it. The little old lady followed her instructions and said 'But I can't.' The receptionist asked whether she could not leave the cabin because the door was too heavy or something was wrong with the handle. 'No there is a Do Not Disturb sign on the door,' she replied. After a moment of silence, as the receptionist realised what had happened, she advised the guest to remove the sign and step into the corridor. The guest followed the instructions and stepped into the corridor but returned somewhat confused. 'I don't understand how I would have disturbed an entire corridor by leaving my cabin. This really has ruined my cruise.'

I will leave that particular beauty with you; however, the Do Not Disturb sign has caused numerous issues like this because quite often, when people step on board a ship they switch off their mind. They are on holiday and the need to think dissolves along with their capacity to navigate or determine direction. There are times when people have put Do Not Disturb signs on their cabins doors, have gone for a stroll around the deck and then have seen the sign and sat outside their cabin waiting for the sign to be removed. They had forgotten that they had put a Do Not Disturb sign there. Finally, there are people who also have fun with Do Not Disturb signs and purposely place them to confuse others. Some put them on the toilet doors, or on other guest's doors for their own entertainment. So imagine you leave your cabin without a sign and then you return and there is a Do Not Disturb sign that you have not put there. What do you do? So you can see the fun in watching that from down the corridor. Little mischievous blighters!

# CHAPTER 48

## THE WONDERFULLY WEALTHY

Isn't it amazing how some people have an aura of wealth? They have an effortless class and elegance that generates a money magnetism. They remind me of the 'Terribly Dignified'; although, this 'Cruise Ship Creature' has a slightly different atmosphere. As they stroll by it is as if a vortex hoovers up money as they pass. You can imagine money fluttering from all over the world in their direction. Yet these people don't need to be too obvious about it. They often wear simplistic attire, albeit being the best quality that can be purchased. What makes them more fascinating is they don't talk about money. They talk about art, they talk about aspirations, culture and music. Yet you know that they are sooooo financially savvy that their private bank accounts are spilling over and they probably use gold bullion to build their houses. What is an interesting learning is that the obviously wealthy don't need to state their wealth, tell people they are wealthy instead there is an inner state of wealth and worthiness that radiates from them. They are often generous and treat people with respect but don't need to behave that way to gain approval – it is just their nature. There are certain cruise ships that tailor specifically to the wealthy and when you witness these creatures in mass, well it is a spectacle to savour. Their interaction is often so dignified and graceful that it is as if one has been transported to an alternative universe where anything and everything is possible. Imagine never considering how much something costs and having no needs. Well this is where these people have arrived in their lives. Many have attained success through contribution to the world and others have had experienced fortuitous events that have enabled them to flourish. Their sense of self-worth is infectious and in many cases they are an inspiration. This is the nice version of the creature. Of course there is also a 'shadow' version which is easy to spot too. These are the ones that use wealth to feel important and ask bar tenders to count how many bubbles are in a fizzy drink. They then demand a fresh one because there are not enough bubbles (this is true – it happened on one of the ships). So, with this 'Cruise Ship Creature' spotting enjoy noticing the two types of wealthy. One is based on ego and the other is based on contributing to the world.

# CHAPTER 49

## THOSE WHO WANT TO APPEAR WEALTHY

There are some who want to appear wealthy yet have an atmosphere of desperation. They are trying to prove themselves by speaking loudly about money and investment. They share unfounded knowledge as though they are experts. They have very definite opinions on how to make money, albeit that it hasn't proven successful. They wear expensive-looking clothes but there is something not quite right. In one particular case there was a chap who was doing his best to appear wealthy to find himself a younger lady on the ship. He would wave cash about and go and gamble in the casino. During his stint on board he lost numerous times on the roulette tables. In fact, there was such a loss that it went to over 100,000 dollars, this was all in order to impress people. Flash the cash which ended up as trash. Unfortunately, this chap couldn't pay his debts and attempted to make an escape from the ship at disembarkation. His rapid departure ended up in a car chase through the disembarkation port's streets. He did all of that to appear wealthy and guess what? He wasn't.

# CHAPTER 50

## THE HAPPY, OBLIVIOUS AND COMPLETELY CHILLED

Some cruisers simply radiate joy, they step onto the ship and all their stress falls from their shoulders. From the moment they enter the cruise terminal they fall into a state of happiness and relaxation. They love the travel, they accept the Captain's Hat brigade and they are simply out to enjoy themselves. Nothing will bother them, nothing will aggravate them because their whole mentality is focused on enjoyment. What you focus your torch on you get more of... so their whole experience from that moment is of being completely chilled.

Now what I find fascinating about this group is that they radiate a certain kind of magnetism. They attract people who are the same kind of happy. Imagine groups of happy people clustering together, all sharing happy experiences. This is what happens with this group and my advice is become one of these because you will have such a lovely time. Every port you go to will be amazing, you will be with people who are up for a good experience and it seems that what you expect you generally get.

With these guests in mind, in Bora Bora there was a trip to a private island. It was an exclusive private island that was accessible only by boat. The tour went to the reef where one could snorkel with a plethora of beautiful fish and then over to the private island for time in hammocks, the opportunity to learn Polynesian dance and a divine buffet that was so tasty that a person could be elevated to blissful states through the taste.

This is where one learns about how people filter the world. On this boat there were two levels so that everyone could enjoy the views. One group went to the top of the boat and others were content to sit on the outer deck on the lower deck. Now it seemed that one group was of the happy and chilled type and the other were of the fault finding kind. Now the fault finders began to grumble because it wasn't terribly sunny. The happy and chilled were content because there was a nice temperature. The fault finders didn't like the fact there were too many fish in the water and it freaked them out. The happy and chilled couldn't believe the abundance and variety of fish that they were able to snorkel with. When the group arrived at the island the fault finders didn't want to learn to dance. The happy and chilled got involved, had a great time with the locals and just loved every moment. The fault finders ate the food quickly and then walked around the island. They said there was nothing there and wanted to end the tour early. The happy and chilled enjoyed the dance, as a group savoured the food, had conversations with the locals about how the food was made and then went for a stroll, a swim and then relaxed in the hammocks. They were relaxed and happy. The fault finding faction demanded to go back to the boat and to return early. So we got everyone together to vote about what would happen next. The fault finders were the minority so the happy and chilled group stayed until the allotted time. The fault finders sat grumpily on the boat and grumbled. It was such an interesting insight into how people filter the world. It seemed that a person could be in paradise and find fault, if that was what they searched for, while the happy and chilled group enjoyed every moment, enjoyed each other's company and when they returned to the boat all sat together saying how much they enjoyed themselves. When you witness a happy group it is worth asking how would you like to experience a cruise and who would you like to be around? In fact if you apply this mentality to life then how would you like to experience the world? This is why I love this 'Cruise Ship Creature' because they are the example of how life can be experienced. Thank you.

PART 5

CHAPTER 51

THE MORE SHOWY CRUISE SHIP CREATURE BREEDS

When we say showy, some people just like to appear and be seen. This little compilation of cruisey creatures are for those who want to be recognised and observed. They make a special effort to be noticed whether it is through posing, perfect physique or how they dress. Time spent observing these types will fuel them because they will feel you admiring them because they have achieved their purpose: to be noticed amongst the mass of fellow cruisers.

CHAPTER 52

THE HOT BODS

Some people work hard on their bodies. They spend hours at the gym, they pay attention to their nutrition and as a result they have the most beautiful bodies that could appear on the cover of magazines. So why would you put in all that work unless you intended to show it off? That is when the 'Hot Bods' take centre stage. This 'Cruise Ship Creature' can be found by the pool or the Jacuzzi. They often seductively remove their outer layers to reveal their bikinis or swimming shorts. In the process of the swimming-pool-strip life pauses and all attention has shifted from the decks to pristine physiques that look as though they have been airbrushed in reality. Lean muscle, six packs and pecks that the top stripper would be proud of cause flushes amongst older women. Those women who have beautiful curves and pert everything cause drool to fall from the mouths of male onlookers. With a slow hair flick, the world is sent back into motion and people return to their routines. Of course it is when the 'Hot Bods' are displaying that many onlookers master the art of not looking, but looking using sunglasses. They appear as though they are looking in one direction while straining their eyes behind sunglasses to look in the other direction. What many don't know is that when the glasses are back-lit the person that you are admiring can see your eyes and what you are up to. Good try!

## CHAPTER 53

## THE 'I AM AN EX-MODEL'

The 'Terribly Dignified' and the 'Hot Bods', with their capacity to evoke brochure imagery, naturally lead to the next 'Cruise Ship Creature': the ex-models. They have the capacity to adopt poses around the ship as though an exclusive magazine photographer will jump out from behind a sun lounger at any moment. When they stroll around the decks you might be misled into thinking they are on a catwalk. When they emerge from the swimming pool you might believe that you are actually watching an advert. These types have somehow managed to maintain themselves against all the forces of nature. Even in their late sixties they still have a youthful glow, the capacity to arrange themselves in fashion sexy poses that transport onlookers into the pages of glossy fashion magazines.

The male versions look like a slightly older version of the men you see on the cover of Men's Health, without airbrushing. They still maintain their six packs and their teeth still defy whiteness. When they smile a small star of light lands precisely on the tooth before their canine. It is uncanny and at the same time the ex-model creatures can cause quite a ruckus. I have witnessed wives belt their husbands who have clearly attempted the art of wearing dark glasses and angling their eyes and their heads so they can look at their ex-model objects of desire whilst appearing to be looking out to sea. Of course that is an art but wives know when husbands are up to that little escapade. Strangely when the flip-flop is on the other foot and the women are salivating at the budgie smuggling ex-model and adopting the same dark-glasses trick why is it that the men don't seem to notice?

# CHAPTER 54

## THE URGENT DECK WALKERS

Of course there is a lot of food on the ship and people on holiday love to take the opportunity to stuff their faces during their waking hours. I always find it astounding how people say 'The more you eat then the more holiday you have for your money'. What they have not considered is the huge amount of weight that a person can gain on a two-week cruise. It is usually around seven pounds or more. At the other end of the scale, are the 'Urgent Deck Walkers'. They do their daily laps and when you open the door on the promenade you have to be careful because you could get mown down. There is nothing that will get in their way. They travel at high velocity and circumnavigate the deck at break-neck speed. They are out there at six in the morning, there for high-paced pounding during sunrises and sunsets. When the wind picks up or the rain pelts down they will continue their speedy stomps. Although there have been times when the storms have been so huge that promenades have been closed off. What do they do then? Well I have witnessed them take to the gym and the treadmills. When those are out of bounds they can be found walking back and forth through the ship and sometimes they do the stairs for an hour or so. When the weather gets really really bad then they will find a way to walk. They have to have a daily constitutional even if it means rebounding off the walls. Please note that these Cruisey Creatures can be mistaken for the 'We Are So Active', yet the prime focus for these creatures is deck walking.

There is an evolved version of this 'Cruise Ship Creature' who will run the decks, even if it is not allowed. On some ships the pounding on the deck vibrates through to the cabins below but they still need to do that run. That way they can enjoy their food and not get fat.

# CHAPTER 55

## THE TERRIBLY DIGNIFIED

Some people exude class, in the same way as the extremely wealthy radiate richness. The 'Terribly Dignified' have the capacity to shine in a classy way and their aura of elegance is captivating. It is as if they have just departed from a game of polo, attended Henley rowing races and then arrive on board the ship. What makes it all the more fascinating is that no matter how they present themselves they just have an air of dignity or class.

Isn't it fascinating how some 'Terribly Dignified' women can wear a sun hat and look as though they have stepped from an exclusive travel magazine? Another woman wearing the same hat can appear as though an unfortunate alien space ship collided with her head that resulted in being dragged through a hedge backwards to meet the spray of a giant muddy puddle as an enormous truck raced through it.

Another insight that may capture your attention is how the 'Terribly Dignified' has an affinity with tweed. At some point during the cruise a tweedy item will appear, especially when the male 'Terribly Dignified' decides to pop up on deck for an evening stroll. The crisp clothing combinations and a sunset provides a sense that the world is a good place and there are chivalrous looking types to admire at sea, from a rather nice sun lounger. The female 'Terribly Dignified' will often accompany her male and has the natural instinct to position herself to increase the 'picture perfect' view of a dignified couple gazing out to sea with a radiant rouge sunset.

What is increasingly astounding about the 'Terribly Dignified' is how they radiate charisma. People are charmed by them as they weave words together like delicate tapestries of pure eloquent wordy joy. The way they walk is dignified, the way they talk is distinguished and there is a miraculous phenomenon whereby their hair remains in perfect position without hairspray. Even their hair is genetically dignified. My advice for when you cross paths with one of these creatures is to absorb as much of their presence as you can because being able to wear tweed or a sunhat and appear as though you are the perfect example of the brochure ideal is a quality that many aspire to.

# CHAPTER 56

## THE SLUG IN THE TUB

What is better than sitting in a hot tub in the sunshine while the ship sails to the Caribbean? The hot tub is a rather amusing territory because there are limited hot tubs for potentially a few thousand passengers to share. So why is it that the hot tub has become exclusive? Rather than accommodate a few people, it is often filled by one giant person who looks like they are a round peg jammed in a bubble-iscious Jacuzzi hole. When I first travelled on ships I thought that maybe the 'Slug In The Tub' was a rare phenomenon; however, the more I sailed on ships, and the more cruises I took, the more I realised that every cruise magically manifested a 'Slug In The Tub'.

So the big question is how do you deal with the 'Slug In The Tub?' The problem is they are usually in the tub the whole day and even into the evening. It seems that when the sun rises the tub slug slithers to the Jacuzzi and plops themselves there. They then reside there for the day and don't leave. I wonder how they visit the toilet. Oh gosh... Why didn't they go for a buffet bonanza? Was it because they were jammed in, or maybe they were amphibians? Had they climbed in and could not get out? Was that why they spent the whole day just sitting appearing to luxuriate in the froth? I guess you could set the fire alarm off to see whether they move; although, if there was a fire then they were in a good place, surrounded by water and in fresh air. They would probably stay in the safety of the tub.

Unfortunately, one can't complain about the 'Slug In The Tub' because they have as much right to be there as anyone else. One might consider the dive bomb option, but there would not be enough spare water to land in. So essentially you would be doing a public body slam and I am sure that could mean that you would be disembarked in the next port or forced to walk the plank while at sea. So after all these deliberations I realised that one requires a very large rubber ring, preferably with a big pink flamingo head on it to stake out a hot-tub-claim and avoid having hot tub company. In addition, you would have to be at the hot tub at the precise moment that the tub is opened – usually around 7.00am. To deter the slug, you may well consider coating the surrounding area in salt to repel the sluggacious creature and buy time to mount the flamingo inflatable. Another consideration – should you want to eat during the day - you will need a very life-like doll in dark glasses to place in that rubber ring while you pop off to get food or honour any toiletry visits. On that particular trail of thought – you may have to come up with a series of distractions to enable the 'quick switch' of the doll and one's self. Of course such antics could be considered a little eccentric; however, if one really has a desire to achieve something out of the ordinary then one has to go to 'thinking outside the hot-tub' mentality.

# CHAPTER 57

## THE DRESS-TASTIC

There is a dress for every occasion and every event in between. This lovely lady holidays on cruises simply to show off the vast array of dresses from her wardrobe. Her life as a fashionista and a 'Dress-tastic' is filled with the joy of dressy display opportunity. What better place to show her stylish wears than on a cruise?

Formal nights fill the 'Dress-tastic' with joy. Within the two cruisey weeks there are usually at least three formal nights for her to take the opportunity to dazzle, sparkle and coordinate jewellery. Shoes that defy understanding decorated with diamante, gold striation or bows resemble decorative ornate foot furniture. You might be forgiven for gazing adoringly at the splendid shoey display that could star in their own Hollywood film: Beauty and the Feet. Quite often this woman travels alone because she does not want to be out-dressily-shone. However, some of these ladies travel with men who choose the classic style so as not to interfere with the 'Dress-tastic's' limelight. There is a rare breed of 'Dress-tastic' who combines forces and as a couple dazzle when they enter the room. Their attire is coordinated perfectly on purpose. They illuminate and enliven every event they attend.

There is a male equivalent to this 'Cruise Ship Creature' where they have a suit for every occasion. Their suits are tailored, have beautiful silk linings and ties that match. When it comes to formal night their tuxedos are individual, tailored and receive numerous compliments. One cruising chap had had tuxedos made from silk and when he entered the room, people admired the exquisiteness behind the creations. One of the oriental silks had two embroidered stalks on the lapel. The outfit was completely original and a beauty. His 'Dress-tastic' skills inspired many who conversed with him based purely on his style.

Other ways that this 'Dress-tastic' type can express itself is in beard decoration. One chap decorated his beard to match his attire. His beard would be red if he was wearing a red tuxedo or a black tuxedo with a red tie and handkerchief. If he wore purple, then his beard would be purple with silver baubles dangling from his facial bushy jutterage. These rare creatures are rather enjoyable to spot especially on formal nights. Within such an event it is wonderful to see who the 'Dress-tastics' are. Even more exciting is to play snap and see whether there are any matching dresses. The greatest pleasure of course would be to wear the ultimate dress and assert yourself as the 'Alpha-Dress-tastic' in the room. What dressy fun!

# CHAPTER 58

## THE HIS AND HERS

Some couples like to let you know they are together. They might hold hands, they may put their arms around each other and canoodle. However, there are the ultimate in 'His' and 'Hers' that need to demonstrate that they are soooo together that you could not possibly think they would ever be apart. Rather than have themselves sewn together to appear like Siamese twins, they come up with more creative solutions. Sometimes it is subtle, they may well wear the same colours. Sometimes they do this without realising it. Other times they wear a similar outfit: white trousers and a similar blue and white striped top. There have been times when I have witnessed couples in that outfit wearing Captain's hats. Yes – back to those bloody Captain's hats! - Yes people go that far and wear the full sailing attire. Sometimes there can even be red dotted cravats or scarfs tied around necks and matching sailory deck shoes. You might consider matching clothes; however, when I saw a couple in gold shell suits and visors, you could not deny that they were together. To make it easier to identify the fact, on the back of the lady's shell suit was written 'Hers' in diamante and on the back of his, he too had 'His' written in swirly writing and yes, it was in diamante too. The pair wore black bum bags, or fanny packs as some call them. On each 'packed fanny' there was 'His' and 'Hers' written again in diamante. As much as these outfits were bizarre, other guests complimented the attire. Admittedly I simply felt general horror. Each day the pair would up their game. It seemed that they had outfits made especially for them to match. When it was Caribbean night she had a dress with a bright Caribbean pattern that perfectly matched his shirt and trousers of the same pattern. When it came to formal night – you guessed it: a tuxedo and matching dress made of the same material. I wondered whether the pair were mad or control freaks. What was sweet was that they held hands, kissed and cuddled a lot. I wondered whether they were simply in love and that Dopamine had fuddled their brains into convincing them that such attire was great. Did the pair have matching underwear with 'His' and 'Hers' on? What if they got mixed up? Would that mean she owned his and he owned hers? The mental churn that accompanied witnessing this couple could be likened to a stampede of wilder beast through a great wilderness. I asked my Officer colleagues for their opinion. Most found it really sweet that the pair, who were in their late sixties, went to such 'His' and 'Hers' efforts for the cruise. Their attire made people go and chat to them and it also made them stand out. After witnessing the 'His' and 'Hers' creature once, I thought that would be the only time. I was wrong. Over the years on ships I have seen similar 'His' and 'Hers' creatures. In some cases, they weren't quite so extreme, simple jackets with 'His' and 'Hers' gave them away. Although the strangest one was when the couple wore t-shirts with the face of their partner on and then on the back of the t-shirt was a picture of the back of the head of their partner. Yes, it was weird but as they sat eating, I wondered how they felt about their own huge face gazing back at them from their partner's chest. Whatever was behind these random acts of 'His' and 'Hers' clothing coordination, you certainly knew that the couple were together. There was no mistaking that and they couldn't accidentally wander off with someone else's partner unless they too wore the same outfit.

# CHAPTER 59

## THE VISOR-TASTIC

On the subject of clothing there seems to be a surge in visors as soon as people arrive on the ship. I understand that people need to shield their eyes and faces from the sun, and the visor is the natural choice rather than a balaclava. Although I don't know how a balaclava would be received on a cruise ship by the other guests. It would be weird to watch someone swim past in such facial attire. There may well be a huge panic or the individual may be arrested and put in the brig. Anyway, I deviate. The truth is there are more visors than you can shake a walking stick at. Some people don't just bring one visor, they bring a whole variety. One particular lady, who had quite a fantastic bouffant, wore a different visor for every day of the cruise. In addition, she had invested in special occasion visors too. The ornamental visory visions varied from gold and glittery to red with diamante and there were some quite lovely designs with Hawaiian flowers decorating them. Admittedly the cruise ship provides people with the opportunity to express themselves amongst complete strangers. There are chances for compulsive liars to invent completely false histories and the occasion for guests to bring a whole suitcase dedicated to hats or visors. It is the perfect place for the 'Eccentric' to be accepted because the staff are forced to talk to them. In the street people would utilise as many different evasion techniques as possible. On the ship the other guests find it amusing and label the more creative sorts or 'unique characters' (weirdos). The random hats or visors enable people something to aspire to and will initiate conversation. I often wonder whether people have a hidden visor fetish that simply needs to be expressed. They use the cruise ship as their head attire debut. That way they can test out and gauge reactions.

On the subject of headwear delicious displays, there has been competitive out-visoring. When you have two ladies who are into their visors, there is opportunity to witness a visor competition. Each day there can be more extreme decoration, which can even result in decorative dangling items. When dangling room ran out, the focus will then evolve into the extreme hair style to display the visor. There were times when the hugest bouffant was forced through the head hole and some rather gravity defying hairstyles incorporating those visory beauties and hair jewellery took centre hair stage. One particular hairstyle resembled an exploded nest with a beaded visor lurking within it. The visor itself could have been considered a bouffant buried treasure. The time and effort made to create such a hairy monstrosity was worthy of an award and the ornate detail was really quite fascinating. Admittedly I was saddened by the fact that I didn't see any budgies residing within the hairy nest. I had hoped that a large bird might land and lay an egg on the creation. It didn't. Shame. The lesson that we can learn from this is that cruising is an opportunity to express yourself and you can gauge the level of reaction according to how many people talk about you or comment on your newly found self-expression. Of course when it comes to being competitive with a visor, in my opinion less is more.

# CHAPTER 60


## THE BOUFFANT BANSHEES


Some of these cruisey creatures can be grouped with the 'Visor-Tastics'; however, they do deserve their own special group because when it comes to formal night there are some phenomenal gravity-defying hair creations that can be likened to great ornately woven sculptures. The wind can be whistling across the deck and this muffy mound will not move.

Of course there are hair raising styles that come from fear, there are those gravity defying creations that are accidental hairy eruptions and there are hairstyles that resemble the ornate weavings of caramel into the shape of an egg attached to a woman's head. When I was a photographer these hairy creations used to fascinate me. If I could align the sun to back-light the colossal coiffure crafting and then fill the face with flash I could create imagery of extreme hair art. I loved it. Strangely the guests loved it too. The illuminated bouffant became 'a thing' amongst the American ladies who cruised on that exclusive ship and no one figured out that I was making these images for my own creative entertainment. How much illumination could one photographer get from the sun setting into a bouffant? Could I capture the sun emerging from the bouffant as if it was setting behind a mountain? I know... I know... I may have worked too many days in a row without a day off by the time I became fixated on hair arrangements. At this time I usually worked around eight months in a row (240 days) without a day off and that does send a person a little loopy). There is something dark and twisted about getting fixated by bulbous bouffant-aciousness, but I did. What made the study of the bouffant bizarity (new word) increasingly exciting is the different bouffant decorations. It was as if a vajazzle had made its way up the body to the head. Where hair was

112

being removed from the nether regions and that region decorated with all manner of glitter and fake jewels, the equal opposite was happening above. Extra hair and extra lift was applied and once that hairy erection was prominently arranged on top of the lady's scalp, it was once again decorated with diamante. On formal nights I would be consumed in photographing smiling women with gravity defying decorated hair. It was wonderful and I soon realised there was a hierarchy of hair. The bigger the bouffant then the greater the hairy female power. It was as if the hair arrangement transformed the lady into a super hairy heroine. In terms of accessories: there were bows, there were beads and there were hair jewels. I felt as though I was in a hairy cruising fairy tale. What more could a creative desire?

# CHAPTER 61

## THE DRESSING GOWNERS

Those who wear dressing gowns need to have a special section dedicated to them. The smokers do have a tendency to wear dressing gowns and slippers on decks early in the mornings, although they are not the only ones. There are those who wear dressing gowns at any time during the day. Some of these 'Cruise Ship Creatures' even have silky dressing gowns or even more elaborate 'dressy' gowns and yes, there are the 'His' and 'Hers' dressing gown wearers. I have witnessed gold brocaded 'His' and 'Hers' written on the back of those gowny beauties. This 'Cruise Ship Creature' observation has been somewhat of an awakening because I never realised there was a hierarchy of dressing gown. In terms of 'Cruise Ship Creatures' these ones are easy to spot. They try to appear as though they spend their lives in the spa. You might see them in their white dressing gown and slippers strolling up and down the stairs in the atrium. Some wear their dressing gown to the pool and make a big show of untying their gowny chords. Others can be found wandering through the spa to the gym or lurking gownily by the spa. We then have the extreme 'Dressing Gowners', who intend to push boundaries so they can see what they can get away with. One of my favourites was the dressing gown at the lunch buffet. There was a little bit of a discussion between the Food and Beverage Managers. What was worse: for them to wear a dressing gown or turn up in budgie smugglers? In the end they let gown wearing go at lunch time; however, when it came to evening that same 'Dressing Gowner' and partner were turned away. There have been 'Dressing Gowners' having a quick go at deck quoits and a couple in the cinema. I have not spotted anyone in a dressing gown at the evening show yet, but who knows? There are always boundaries to be pushed and opportunities to flaunt a dressing gown. I have not seen a formal dressing gown yet but have witnessed a very well made smoking jacket and cravat. That snuck into the formal night gathering because it was made of silk.

The final and my most favourite dressing gown episode was with a rather rebellious lady who liked her drink. She was on what we call a 'booze cruise' or as was listed earlier as a party cruise, which is a short cruise of around four days. As mentioned before, the party cruises usually visit ports such as Amsterdam or Zebrugge. This particular cruise went to Guernsey and while we were on a tender I had to ask this particular lady to put her nipples away for health and safety reasons. It is at times like these I wonder what on earth the cruising industry is coming to and how weird life is in general. The particular lady was somewhat inebriated and felt it necessary to lift up her top and press her bare breasts against the tender window for the Officers on the quayside to see. At first she refused to put away the guilty nipples but I advised her of all the locations she could cut her nipples. It was only then that she kindly covered them up. She was quiet for a while, like a naughty girl. When I walked away she burst into a drunken song. I had to then advise her that as much as her singing voice might appeal to some, it was better that she refrained in the confined space of the tender because it may aggravate the other guests.' When the tutting began by the guests, she finally stopped. So what has this got to do with dressing gowns? Well on the day of disembarkation this lady had to leave the ship in a very small set of pyjamas. We gave her a dressing gown because she had cleverly packed her suitcase the night before and forgotten to leave out her travelling clothes. During the night her suitcase was transported to the terminal and in the morning she realised that she only had her rather skimpy pyjamas to disembark in. Those pyjamas certainly didn't leave much to the imagination so the ship provided a dressing gown and slippers so that she didn't get arrested for indecent exposure. I have to admit that the situation tickled me. Erectus Nipplus Maximus.

# CHAPTER 62

## THE RICH MAN AND YOUNG WOMAN

There are certain ships that attract these 'Cruise Ship Creatures'. Not surprisingly they are the more luxurious ships within the cruising industry. The happy wealthy chappy can show off to his delightful young thing while showing her off to the other men on the ship. The charming gold-digging commodity will behave as though she is in some travel magazine shoot and wear all her wafty clothes, large brim hats and bikinis that reveal taught, youthful flesh. She will be attentive and look stunning on formal nights. It will be the rich man's dream, it is what he has worked for – all that success and he can buy a 'beautiful bird'.

My favourite example of this was a man in his late seventies, who liked to wear leopard skin budgie smugglers, or as my great friend said 'It looks like wet sand in a sock.' Anyway this chap wore his rather small speedos and suffered from flatulence. Yep, he was rich and posteriorly wafty. His 'wife' was a beautiful Russian in her mid-thirties with a body that made men walk into things or simply have to cover their laps in her presence. When I say beautiful, this woman was stunning. Her smile would light up a room and she had a certain natural elegance about her. She could have chosen any wealthy man, although this was 'her' wealthy man. That wealthy man created a jet stream of flatulence as he swam across the pool. Where the pool was calm it was transformed into a Jacuzzi as he jetted across. She would wear her large brim sun hat and lie beside the pool waving contentedly at her rich man. She was fascinating, he was happy and the other guests were curious. Was she his granddaughter, his daughter or his wife?

# CHAPTER 63

## THE ODD OUTFITS GROUP

Talking of outfits, there are some rather bemusing attires often paraded around decks and particularly on formal nights. What makes them all the more fascinating is that most of them are actually purposeful. In addition, there are some people that clearly have emerged from the 70s, 80s or 90s. I have seen people who look like they have escaped from the set of Dallas, others who were fully clad in safari wear taking a stroll on deck. Of course there are the standard 'Hello I am a sailor' gang who wear blue and white striped jumpers and navy shorts. That is usual. As mentioned before there are the leopard skin lovers and the leather wearing luvvies. All of them are fun to spot, and then there are older ladies that have a skill for wearing highly decorated tent-like skirts. The level of billowy-ness per inch is quite a wonder. It is always amusing watching the wind pick up these wafty wonders and lift them as they totter about the promenade deck. When the wind is high these little ladies are transformed into human sails and can be blown around deck at a rapid pace without even trying. One of the peculiar things I witnessed was a lady bending over in such a dress, it blew over her head. As she struggled to pull it down her arm positioning was miscalculated and that dress literally blew off her body. It was like watching a large sheet flying across the sky and there she was in her rather large knickers, bra and sandals. Kindly someone offered her a towel while others stood looking dumbfounded by how such a situation evolved from nowhere. As they say 'Worse things happen at sea!' This leads on to the next 'Cruise Ship Creature' – the 'Naked Accidentals'.

## CHAPTER 64

## THE NAKED ACCIDENTALS

Many people like to sleep naked, the sense of naked freedom makes the state so appealing. However, when cruising on a ship it is generally wise to wear something during the night because ships are more vulnerable to incidents. Take for example if the ship runs into trouble or has a fire then the naked people are generally more at risk of hypothermia, nether region frostbite or barbequed sausage syndrome, especially if mister naked accidentally strolls into a flamey inferno, sausage first.

Quite a common incident is when a guest-of-the-naked-kind forgets where they are and needs the bathroom during the night. In their half-asleep state they select the wrong door and step out into the corridor, before they know it the door has closed behind them. Their first reaction is to hammer on the door but unfortunately the hubby or wifey is wearing earplugs. Awkward? Naked... Drafty? Sooo what do you do? Well you have to go to reception to ask someone to open the door. Depending on what deck you are staying on and the distance from reception, makes the journey more interesting. Ideally one would prefer the naked streak to be as short as possible, and without the need to pass through public spaces like the central atrium. Also the naked dash would be easier if one already knew the layout of the ship because being lost and naked may well result in huge emotional trauma. Imagine stumbling into the disco or taking a wrong turn and ending up naked on stage. It is possible because the ship has numerous secret doors and corridors.

Survival and inventiveness are the 'Naked Accidental's' friend. On some floors there are launderettes and linen cupboards. This is where the 'Naked Accidental' can utilise their body coverage inventiveness. On some floors there are floral arrangements and a number of nakeds have shown up at reception with a decorative floral arrangement about their person. It is amazing how the

118

positioning of large Lilly can save the day. Others have found towels in linen cupboards while others have created their own personal sandwich board from pictures they have prized from walls. It is remarkable how a half-asleep naked moment of panic provides all manner of body coverage inspiration. A number of 'Naked Accidentals' have made their way to the gym to pick up a towel, which is quite logical; however, to get to the spa and gym they usually have to traverse a number of floors and make their way to the front of the ship.

Christmas decorations have made a rather beautiful body adornment with baubles hanging from protruding places and Rudolf taking on the genital covering reindeer role. Father Christmas and his white beard have been known to cover a portly posterior. Other 'Naked Accidentals' have not been so lucky and have been witnessed on deck prizing life-rings from the railing to cover their credentials. Unfortunately the life ring often has escaping appendages popping through the hole. All in all, the reception staff, the night staff and housekeeping have witnessed sights that will haunt them for the rest of their lives. In such an unexpectedly naked situation the easy alternative would be to find the phone in the corridor, call reception and utilise the stay-put approach while scouting the linen cupboard for any material to cover one's self. Alternatively knock on your neighbour's door and ask for help. Of course that wouldn't create a decent story.

# CHAPTER 65

## THE INTENTIONALLY NAKED

Well since there are the accidental nakeds there are also those who are 'Intentionally Naked'. In fact, the whole guest population have been known to be naked... Imagine... or maybe not – it wasn't terribly inspiring. I referenced this earlier; however, here is the detail. There were thousands of wobbly, hairy bottoms to be seen in all directions. Basically the ship was chartered by a nudist holiday company. For two weeks in the Mediterranean there was a flesh-fest in all directions. To make matters stranger is that the crew had the option to be naked. Now obviously naked crew would raise a few questions. How would you determine an Officer's rank? Of course the Officers could wear hats and brocade and shoes. Some people suggested that socks with stripes may provide the answer. My suggestion was body paint to paint on the stripes. The question then was raised where would the stripes be painted? As is standard in the wardroom, the discussion descended into ridicularity and of course the Captain's appendage was the key area to paint stripes on. In the end the crew decided to keep their clothes on, simply to demonstrate the division between guests and crew. A few had considered the naked antics; however, painting the ship with no clothes could be a challenge. Or serving food and running in and out of the galley could certainly cause some real health and safety issues especially with flambé or grills.

For those who are curious about how this works – embarkation involved the guests arriving clothed. Once on board they could cast aside any clothing and prance about the ship in all their naked glory. The 'Intentionally Naked' guests are provided with a small handkerchief that they take with them all over the ship. That small square of material is to sit on because sweaty bottoms on chairs will tarnish them, also the potential for the intermingling of bodily fluids around the ship provides health and safety issues.

What you may not have considered is that the Jacuzzis had to be cleaned more regularly because there was an increase in 'activity' amongst the guests and it wasn't to cool down. The shows were more of a challenge for the entertainment cast because a standing ovation was not a pleasant sight and somewhat off-putting. Imagine a thousand naked people all standing up simultaneously to celebrate your show. One of the Cruise Directors wound up the cast saying that since it was a naked cruise the cast would have to perform naked. It was then realised how important all the costumes were to give the show pizazz. The world of cruising naked strangely became normal after a week because people were lined up for the buffet naked or as we called it in the buff buffet. Guests promenaded about the decks without any clothy items and the gym had increased wobble due to lack of Lycra or support bras. People played bridge and attended craft classes in the buff. Amongst the crew, deck quoits got renamed dick quoits, shuffleboard became renamed shuffle–cock and table tennis became known as table penis. Now imagine the amount of cleaning that would have to take place. The good thing for the nudists was that they could sunbathe without the tan line issue (unless they wore socks and sandals). PLEASE NOTE: That A Socks And Sandals Creature Is Detailed Within The Guide)

Thinking back it was a random experience for the whole crew. When the new passengers embarked with clothes on and kept them on something seemed oddly strange about the new passenger phenomenon.

PART 6

CHAPTER 66

THE DOWN AND DIRTY CRUISE SHIP CREATURES

This section is not going to be terribly pleasant because it references intestinal smogs, posterioral protrusions and purposeful bottomy intentions. The unfortunate truth is there are some really malicious individuals who will purposely pop-a-poo-in-a-public-place and others who may achieve the same goal unintentionally. In my opinion, it is worth being aware of these cruisey creatures because you don't want to be trapped in a lift with them or get stuck in a confined space. At the end of the section I felt it only fair to show you how the ship's crew become nasal 'Super Heroes' to resolve the below. You will learn how huge the power of brocade on an Officer's shoulder has over their subordinates.

# CHAPTER 67

## THE PHANTOM BLOW OFF

A blow off is not pleasant in any sense of the word. It just isn't. People always find their own creations funny and others are generally repulsed; however, there is a breed of person who is purposeful with their flatulence. Honestly I have never witnessed so many noises that sounded as though a duck had been trodden on, squashed or kicked as I have on cruise ships. Obviously the rich food and the increased food intake has an effect on the most resilient intestine. Yet there is a common 'Cruise Ship Creature' who will go and blow off in a lift knowing that people on the other decks will walk into that monstrosity at full fruition. Another phantom farter would walk through the bridge class when they were in full concentration; pass wind and pass on. There were occasions when the cinema was at full capacity; he would lurk at the back, wait for the film to start and then make a stink and disappear. The 'Phantom Blow Off' would wait for the Captain's Welcome Aboard Party and as the people were happily gathered, create a love puff and then float away. Just when the Captain came to a joke delivery the crowd were gagging on the stench.

The Officers on the ship became very aware of the phantom because some of us worked in offices which were shielded from the corridor by a curtain. There were times that the phantom slightly opened the curtain, blew off into the office and then left the workers in the confined space to deal with the atmospheric repercussions. A couple of times I was alerted to his presence because I heard a strange duck squashing sound. As soon as I dashed towards the curtain, he was gone. I discussed the issue with the Security team because I felt that it was a criminal act to confine people in a space and pass wind at them. I wanted the phantom disembarked. The Security team took the issue seriously and made investigations; however, the bugger was clever and we could not tell who he was. He had figured out how to merge with the crowd, drop a methane bomb and leave without detection. He was a master at his fart and his skill at being a phantom was extraordinary. He always left undetected.

Now before people consider the fact I reference a chap being stink sexism. There was a very glamorous woman who wasn't quite a phantom because her dastardly stink escapades were discovered. Admittedly her disguise was quite astounding. You would never have believed that a woman who wore so many sequins on formal night, or had hair so immaculately arranged could create a destructive smog that trail blazed behind her. To make it worse her smooth-stinkaceous move was on the dance floor. As she flitted about in the arms of a gentleman host numerous little gifts would be shared for the other dancers to inhale. One couple doubled over as they coughed after a surprise waft caught them completely off-guard. It just goes to show you can't judge a book by its cover and you can't judge a glamorous 'Cruise Ship Creature' by beautiful attire when a stench lurks beneath the sequin-clad ballgown.

# CHAPTER 68

## THE TOILET BLOCKER

I didn't really want to get into these shadow cruise ship-shitty types. These are like the Darth-toilet-invaders of the 'Cruise Ship Creatures'. They would be the ones that people did their best to avoid. My original plan was to focus on the amusing, the random and the easy to spot, plus a few really obvious ones. Although, when talking to my friends, they were most curious about the phantom, this one and the 'Code Browner'. Note to self: I must pick friends who have slightly different interests.

The 'Toilet Blocker' is an elusive creature. You would never know who this creature was. You will only know when they have caused yet another blockage by the fact that the whole toilet system ceases working. Cruise ships have a fragile toilet system. The pipes are small and not designed for anything that is not tissue or the standard human delivery. When I say standard, I mean there are limits.

So 'Toilet Blocker' … You would assume that the sign on the toilet that states there should just be tissue and human excrement down the toilet was obvious, so why would you put a number of tea bags down the toilet? That seems a little odd right, but when a rubber duck blocks the system you wonder what has gone on in the cruise ship world. What many people, who have not worked behind the scenes, do not know is that on some ships there is a daily ship plumbing report specifically targeting toilet blockages. We, in our amusement, call this the ship 'shit' report. Every morning the ship's Officers are advised of the plumber's toiletry discoveries. The rubber duck did make a name for itself because on the ship most of the time you have a shower. The rubber duck itself is designed for floating in a bath, so what the heck was the person thinking when playing with ducky on the toilet? Consider the number of flushes involved in getting that unsuspecting ducky down the tube. There was a discussion in the Officer's mess about the fact that the guest must have simply wanted to float the rubber duck on something and then accidentally flushed it. A number of us disagreed because you would have to intentionally flush the little ducky dude. We will never know because the duck was in a transition pipe which was fed by numerous toilets. It isn't as if you can walk up to each cabin and ask if the guests had misplaced their rubber duck down the potty.

There was an incident where a constant complainer kept blocking the toilet. He would block the toilet and then complain that the toilet was blocked. He wanted money back because constant toilet blockage was unacceptable. The plumber was at his wits end. Finally, the plumber said that the guy must have a medical problem because basically he was the cause of the blockages on a daily basis. When the Hotel Operations team advised the guest of their rather unfortunate findings, the constant complainer said he felt victimised because he did indeed have a medical problem and felt that his toilet should be specifically adapted to accommodate his anal issue.

# CHAPTER 69

## THE CODE BROWNER

This 'Cruise Ship Creature' is a menace. They have taken it one step too far when it comes to the shit issue. If there is a random turd found anywhere on the cruise ship it is called a code brown. We have to radio the issue through, cordon off the area and get in a swat cleaning team. Or, as we call them, the shit swatters. It isn't as if this team have people dressed as Ninjas abseiling in on a turd, instead they wear white, have face masks and gloves. What always amazes me is that the tape used to surround the turd is crime scene tape. Yes, I know... It is technically a crime scene and is treated as such. There were numerous code brown issues; however, a few spring to mind. Imagine the audacity of someone balancing their turd on a bronze sculpture in the art gallery. Honestly, someone with a purposeful intent actually took a turd on a little ship tour from the toilet to the gallery and placed it in the hand of a bronze sculpture of a ballerina with her hand outstretched. So how long did it take for anyone to notice? Well it was actually a couple of days because there were reports of an atrocious anal aroma; however, it was only when one of the guests noticed the ballerina had an additional and unusual feature that the code brown was discovered. The comment that went with the discovery was 'Quite clearly the art you are selling is shit!' The art gallery was transformed into a crime scene and the all surfaces in near vicinity were scrubbed. When investigated Security could not discern who the culprit was because the CCTV cameras were not pointing at that particular sculpture.

Another infamous 'Code Browner' kept delivering his brown creations into the lift. Imagine... THE LIFT. People would step in the lift unaware of the code brown awaiting their feet. The lift door would close and the victim would be in the confined space with no escape. Sometimes there were a few poos dotted around or sometimes one cleverly tucked in the corner. Unfortunately, when the lift-spattered mess was walked around the ship. So again the swat team would be called in. Since the lifts were see-through the 'Code Browner' would draw full attention as the SWAT team cleaned while the lifts continued to be called to different floors. One particular time a guest mistook the crime scene tape and thought that the lift was the place of a murder scene and that was when the rumours began. Since the launderette is the place for gossip mongers and if one of those lovely ladies or gentleman witness anything suspect they scurry to the launderette to create a huge rumour. In this case it may well have been that someone died due to turd torment.

The final case that I will share with you is the one that bemused me the most. Obviously there are a lot of these code brown situations to reference over the years; however, this code brown was beyond all comprehension. Basically the 'Code Browner' went all out for destruction. This is the ultimate malicious code brown that was planned to precision. The browns were placed on the running treadmills in a gym in such a way that they created individual skid marks on each machine. The mess was caught up in the mechanism too. The seats on the bikes were brown so the code browns were placed on the bike seats so people sat on them if they were not paying attention. Little browns were placed on the foot plates of the cross trainers too. How often do you study the foot plates of cross trainers? There was a brown folded into a yoga mat and a couple placed on kettle bells. When those kettle bells swung the acrobatic poop flew too. After the gym the 'Code Browner' decorated the male changing room with a purposeful smiley face made of brown. We assumed the culprit was a male, although it could have been a clever decoying female who snuck into the male changing room and thought she would create a turdular emoji. You would have thought it would have stopped there but no... The culprit went into the spa and placed the turds on the marble hot beds and then put brown hand marks all over the walls. To finalise the brown destruction, she or he tossed a couple of brown floaters into the hydro-pool. There was rumour that those browns were melted Snicker bars but in truth, who was going to taste them?

Finally, the culprit wrote on the spa wall 'This ship is shit' - in shit. The person was clearly full of shit or had collected it to go to shit town on the ship. In terms of crime scene: Security could not find the culprit again because you don't have cameras in the changing rooms, the spa hot bed area was also without camera and the gym cameras were faulty. Since everyone was astounded by the volume of shit the rumour became that melted Snickers had been sculpted and used to finalise the shit fest in the spa. I think the thing that got me with this 'Cruise Ship Creature' was the sheer venom and planning that had been made to deliver such a code brown conundrum. If discovered they would have been disembarked instantly. Yet that was what was amazing – they delivered and remained undetected.

# CHAPTER 70

THE GOLDEN BROCADE OF POWER...

AND THE SHIP SUPER HEROES WHO COMBAT CRETINOUS CRUISE SHIP CREATURES

Okay this bit has snuck in, but it has to be written to enable faith in the shippy superheroes who save the guests from other passenger's intestinal doom! This one story literally captivated me for hours and for the duration of the contract I kept referring back to it in terms of how much power a person could have due to brocade.

So back to the 'Golden Brocade of Power' ... Admittedly this isn't really a 'Cruise Ship Creature' but I had to pop this in to this book for my own amusement and to record it for posterial posterity. Quite often, on the older ships, the toilets block very easily and there are phantom aromas around and about the decks. The problem is that the toilets don't flush like usual toilets, instead they are based on vacuums. The system of pipes is complex and often crack with time. So a mysterious stinkacious smog can turn up and lurk on deck while the origin may not be easily traced. While I was working on one particular ship, I sat opposite the Housekeeping Manager who had been phoned regarding a stinky complaint. It was then I witnessed the true power of three brocade stripes on an epaulette. Imagine overhearing a phone call that goes like this: 'Can you send three Housekeeping Officers to deck eight mid-ship to advise how bad the reported stink is there. I want three of you so that we can gauge an average of the smell and maybe locate the origin. Can you report back to me as soon as possible?'

About ten minutes later the following conversation continued 'So you all agree it is 8/10 on stink level? Oh... so... you can't determine the origin. Have you sniffed all the walls and the floors in the area?'

There was a pause while he listened to their response and considered what the next course of action was. 'Okay... You think it must be the toilets and the aroma has somehow been displaced? That would make sense. Can you please sniff the walls because then we can advise the plumber of potential locations.' When you hear a conversation like that it is very easy to question whether you are actually appearing on some kind of joke television show. When the Housekeeping Manager put down the phone he noticed me staring at him with a bemused expression on my face. 'Are you okay?' he asked.

I was okay in a somewhat puzzled way. 'I think I have just witnessed true power,' I replied.

He did not seem to understand what I was saying. 'How is that?' he asked.

'You have the power to call three people to go and sniff a fart. That is true power.'

He smiled, he had not even thought of that because such incidents were his 'normal'.

'On top of that, after they have graded the fart aroma, they then sniffed walls and floor areas to determine the stink origin. That is power. The power to request for people to sniff a stench is amazing but to then ask them to sniff walls and floors to locate the stinky source is beyond anything I could ever comprehend!' I said.

As always his usual response to my completely mystified comments was a smirk and a nod. In that moment he realised he had true shippy power. It was amazing what a bit of gold brocade on an epaulette could do for a person, especially in the stinky arena.

## PART 7

## CHAPTER 71

## THE DANGEROUS CRUISE SHIP CREATURES

Some of the 'Cruise Ship Creatures' are actually dangerous. This section contains those who can cause physical harm and those who can produce psychological harm. The creatures listed below may well lull you into a false sense of security, so when spotting and engaging with the below types, always be on your guard, have a back-up escape route and have a code word with your partner that will make it very clear that it is time to leave.

# CHAPTER 72

## THE WALKING STICK WHACKERS AND DUELLERS

Oh the power of the walking stick. Who would have thought that an item used as a walking support could sneakily be used as a weapon? A sneaky whack to the back of the knee and the victim can face-plant on plush carpet. So... considering there are the sneaky walking stick prodders, and those who appear like they did not intend to trip someone up... leads me to those who are grumpy, aggressive and confrontational. Something that I have witnessed (in the confined cruisey atmospheres) is that unpleasant people don't develop pleasantness the older they get. In fact, they seem to master the art of growing more unpleasant. Now imagine two rather unpleasant people in a confined space wielding walking sticks... What if those two unpleasant people decided to have an 'unpleasantry-off'. You see when people feel entitled they often feel more entitled than the next person. If you have two unpleasant people feeling more entitled than the other, then that is when walking stick duelling can take place. Two rather grumpy men, a foyer and a heated discussion about who was going to have the last canapé meant rather than locking horns that they locked walking sticks. Before you knew it, the Jedi 'Walking Stick Duellers' had emerged and two wives stood looking rather baffled when suddenly one of their husbands adopted a fencing pose and prodded the other who defended himself as though he was one of the Jedi himself. To make the situation more extreme both were in their eighties and had hearing aids... So when they insulted each other it was rather loud and neither could actually hear the other. As the duel descended into a walking-stick-tastic frenzy a crowd gathered, as though two old gentlemen swishing walking sticks in the air was part of the entertainment. Other walking sticks twitched on the edge of the circle until Security were called. I am always amazed by how bored the Security Officers look by some of the more random sights that can be witnessed on a ship. He certainly had seen it all before.

'Gentleman, lower your walking sticks!' he said.

Neither could hear him.

'Gentleman, Lower Your Walking Sticks!' He shouted.

The pair paused, glanced at each other and then became grumpy best buddies. They turned and glanced at Security and sized him up. When the Gurkhas arrived the grumpy old gentlemen were outnumbered and the walking sticks were lowered.

'Gentleman you have a choice... You make up or we put you in the brig,' Security said calmly.

The pair glanced at each other, shook hands and went their separate ways. What they didn't know was that Security would be watching them on the CCTV because as soon as there was any more trouble they would be disembarked from the ship.

# CHAPTER 73

## THE MISTRESS

There have been some very awkward situations involving mistresses. There are the standard situations where a man takes his mistress on holiday. That is obvious and not terribly exciting to talk about. There are many situations where the most unexpected chap has a real beauty on his arm. She is half his age and wearing cheese wire to hold the nipple tassel bikini together. It is apparent how much she is enamoured by his personality because she laughs at everything he says and gazes at him adoringly. Of course we can't pass judgement because no doubt she paid to be there herself and is a keen business woman. I might be being a little bit sarcastic. Although there is the equal opposite where an older woman brings along her very attractive young man who has a *Men's Health* body and the personality of a sprout. So now that we have that out of the way... There are two stories that really captivated me. The first was on my first ship where a woman kept going to the photography department and buying all the pictures of a couple on the ship. When the couple went to find their pictures they were never there. The wife was unaware that her husband had a mistress and 'The Mistress' would sit in the same room or on the deck away from the couple but where the chap could see her. She would make sure she looked stunning and simply be in the room or in close proximity. Of course the chap had to try his hardest not to react or respond. After a few days 'The Mistress' became more calculating and purposely appeared in the back of photographs and purchased a copy but made sure another copy was left for the couple. In the end the husband made a request for the Captain to intervene. It was a challenging situation and 'The Mistress' was called in to find out what was going on. It turned out that the chap had said that he was divorced and she found it to be untrue. He then said that he planned to leave his wife for 'The Mistress'. He had promised to take her on a cruise. She realised it was all lies and when she found a cruise catalogue in his car with a cruise circled, she decided to book herself on that cruise and make him uncomfortable. She did not intend to upset the wife or confront her. The Captain asked her to stop what she was doing and she did, to the relief of the husband, until the final day. 'The Mistress' decided that the wife had to know what a despicable man her husband was and introduced herself to the wife in the laundrette of all places. She told her who she was and that she did not want to ruin her cruise; however, she had been having an affair with her husband and she should know. The wife was distraught and asked for her own cabin. We assumed that was the end of their marriage. 'The Mistress' finished with the chap and would you believe this? She met a single chap on board. The pair had been dance partners. They paired up and became repeat regular cruisers who 'Just Loved To Dance'.

The other story, which again was fascinating to me, was a chap who had a mistress and paid for her to be on board while he was on the ship with his wife. He would visit 'The Mistress' during the night. He would sneak out of his cabin wearing his pyjamas... go and rock the boat and then return. I remember hearing that the chap had advised Security that he had a very bad case of sleep-walking and was renowned for it. When they followed him on the CCTV cameras, it seemed that he had a very bad case of sleep-walking that led him to a specific cabin at the other end of the ship on a nightly basis. The wife remained completely unaware.

To balance this out let's talk about the hot 'mister' with the cougar... There have been a number of ladies who have sported beautiful young men on their arms. At first you wonder whether they brought their son along with them but no, it is quite apparent there were more explicit liaisons taking place. Quite often these women are self-made and have an extreme elegance and look blooming good for their age. Some of the fifty year olds could be mistaken for thirty year olds until you have a sneak preview of their birthdate on the system. It is obvious that they have taken care of themselves, have a real sense of style and are actually in their late forties or mid-fifties. There are cases of women in their seventies with men twenty years their junior and well done them! Of course the ladies in their late forties and fifties are easier to spot and most likely to parade their younger lovers. These ladies lounge by the pool (sometimes in their leopard skin bikinis) and beside them the hottest chap you can imagine flexes his pecs and has a six pack that was so defined that you wondered whether it had been grafted on. I had a conversation with one lady, who was a self-made millionaire, who had a wonderful attitude. She said 'Well men do it and in this age of equality would I prefer to peer at a fat middle-aged snoring man or have passionate sex with a young man who wants to experience the world? I know what most women would answer. Obviously I get looks from other women, I would guess that was envy, but I know they would love to be in my situation. Some of the men scowl at me... no idea why. What has fun with a young man got to do with them? Why do I care anyway? Oh I guess I must be giving their wives an insight into what is possible and it may inspire men to take more care of themselves.'

# CHAPTER 74

## THE STEWARD /STEWARDESS OPPORTUNISTS

There are definitely some rather strange people that sail on ships. Some of these 'Cruise Ship Creatures' cross the boundaries and take complete advantage. When you talk to the cabin stewards you will be astounded by the weird and wonderful requests made. Here is one that will disturb you. So imagine this, a woman in her late seventies who, was not so nimble, would call her cabin steward and ask him to help her to her feet. When he put his hands under her arms she would fall backwards and pull him onto the bed on top of her. There were times that she attempted to kiss him. When this cabin steward told me about this I was astounded. Admittedly he was a handsome chap; however, he had had single women travellers offering to pay for certain services that were not listed in the brochure or on the menu. There have been times when he has been called to a cabin and the female guest emerged from the shower in her birthday suit and it was not her birthday and there was no suit. It wasn't just women making the financial offers, there were elderly chaps making such requests too. I asked what he did about it. He said that he politely refused and if the guest persisted then he would request to be moved to a different section of the ship. That was his last option because he would lose the tips from the other guests that he had been taking care of.

# CHAPTER 75

## THE SWIMMING POOL PESTS

Previously I mentioned the 'Slug In The Tub', the person who blocks the whole whirlpool or Jacuzzi using their whole body mass. Where the 'Slug In The Tub' lounges, the 'Swimming Pool Pests' are an entirely different fast-paced breed. This lot are hardy, focused and will make sure that if you cross their swimming path then they will mow you down with a swift punch disguised as front crawl. I have witnessed leg pulling and accidental slaps around the head as they swim past. There are dastardly swimming tricks taking place to territorialise an area of water.

Of course there are always the swimming ladies, who do not like to get their hair wet. When the 'Swimming Pool Pest' is in the water an unexpected swimming pool tidal wave will catch these unsuspecting ladies from behind and give them a super soaking. The pest will swim underwater to remain undetected and appear as though the suspicious soaking was nothing to do with them. The pests are both genders, they usually wear swimming hats and goggles from the moment they step on deck. That way they can't be identified and can live a double pool-pest identity.

Talking of disguises, we also have to be aware of extreme swimming hats. My favourite had a shark fin on the back. That particular swimmer became known as the shark because he was a pool predator of the worst kind. He would not let anyone swim in 'his' imaginary lane. When he finished his workout, he would then prowl the periphery for ladies that he might wish to devour. Can you imagine, as a woman, you are innocently floating by the edge of a pool and a man in a shark-finned swimming hat circles you like potential sharky prey? Random? Weird? Great fun to watch.

On the subject of swimming hats, some swimming hats resemble bowls of fruit and others a Caribbean island. If you are not fully functioning in the morning you might mistakenly believe a fruit salad has taken to the pool for an early morning dip. Other than random swimming hat displays there are some quite fascinating swimming attires. Some are disturbing while others are just simply a load of strings holding some very small pieces of material. The swimming pool is a great place for spotting many a variety of 'Cruise Ship Creature' because it is the equivalent of the watering hole. In addition to swimming you can notice purposeful bending over by the pool, generally odd positioning and ping pongs flying from unexpected places. When a bowling ball rolls along the deck then maybe it has gone a step too far!

# CHAPTER 76

## THE TABLE TENNIS MENACE AND QUOITS QUIRKIES

Some people are competitive and they just can't help it. It seems that something in their nature makes them that way. So when an innocent game of table tennis transforms into old people in sandals and socks belting table tennis balls at each other, you might be a little better prepared. You might laugh at the concept of being belted with a ping pong but it is a serious matter.

For those that don't know: the game of table tennis involves the usage of small bats (paddles) and light-weight balls. Of course there is the table and a height-challenged net. Hence the name table tennis. I often wonder who came up with such an activity. I bet when the idea was conceived that the creator had no idea how a sweet old granny could turn into a table tennis hustler. There she was sweetly sitting beside the table tennis group doing a bit of crochet and then she 'innocently' offered to join in to make up the numbers. As soon as she lifted the 'paddle' you noticed her eyes transform from cute with crochet to bat-wielding-warrior-ess, oh and with a distinct assassin's gaze. When she handled the ping and ponged the ball at unsuspecting players with venom, you knew the inner competitor had risen and she intended to win. A gentle and fun game became a competition of Olympic magnitude as the old chaps gathered together in support of one another. There is no way they were going to be 'chicked' by the crochet countess. What made it particularly attention-grabbing was the sudden appearance of sweat bands. During the leisurely game there were no such items; however, when the old dear got the guys going a sudden supply of sweat bands magically appeared.

So there we are: Mabel has mauled the manly mob with a ping pong ball and suddenly other ladies got wind (some have wind anyway) of the phenomenon taking place. The men lined up and were sent game after game with their tail between their legs. All the while the entertainment host tries to calm any hostilities. When the next loser crumbled he threw his ping pong paddle on the floor in the same way as John McEnroe because it should not be so ping pongyly serious! A fun game descended into a competitive catastrophe as Mabel mobilised all her skills and wiped the floor with her competitors. She took the prize and smiled with graceful delight and returned innocently to her crochet creation. Unfortunately, there was an exhausted array of old chappy carnage dotted about the deck. In the end someone asked Mabel if she had played before. She smiled sweetly, oh yes – I used to compete for the British team. A beautiful moment for the onlookers, those jammed in the Jacuzzi and others who were stuffing their face with food from the grill making it their tenth meal of the day.

In the meantime, deck quoits usually had quite a turn out. It seemed that during days at sea the quoiters increased in numbers. Maybe a weird type of quoiting cloning was going on in the cabins. Cabin clones... Hmmm. Anyway, for those that don't know what deck quoits is well it is essentially lobbing circles of rope across the deck. The whole point of the game is to throw a ring of rope across a grid painted onto one of the cruise decks. There are usually a few painted grids because the game is surprisingly popular. It apparently originated from people hurling horse shoes. When these games descend into chaos, and they do, especially if a few cocktails have been involved, then it is better to have a facial collision with a bit of rope than a metal horse shoe. Also if you think about it logically it is easier to make another quoit of rope when there are plenty of ropes on cruise ships. That is, unless horses have taken to going on world cruises, there would only be a certain amount of horse shoes available for throwing.

With regards to the 'Quoites Quirkies', it is worth going along for a watch or even taking part. What I personally found amazing is how so many of the 'Quoites Quirkies' have a tendency to wear tops with horizontal blue and white stripes and in the quoiting quirky group there is an increased number of Captain's style hats per head than the general Captain's hatty average about the ship. After that little deviation you might notice that at first the game appears innocent but then there will be those who are competitive. The entertainment host has to really pay attention because there are those fixated on scores and are desperate for that prize certificate. Strangely the more sea days there are then the more serious the 'Quoites Quirkies' get with the game. At times you wonder whether the sea air makes them a little bit odd because when you see someone throwing all the quoits out of the box you realise that someone has lost it!

# CHAPTER 77

## THE VICTIMS

There are victims of life and those who love to play 'The Victim'. I have witnessed 'victim –off' at a number of formal dinners. This is where people share their woes and out woe each other – there are of course the 'Out Woers' which are a specific creature. They have their own special woeing section. Back to the 'Victims' - if someone had a cold then another had the flu. If something bad happened to one, then another had experienced something far worse. During the description there is always an increase in general rasping emphasis. The 'Victim' is an interesting architype and the unfortunate truth on a ship is that there is a captive audience. One can't get away unless they plan on jumping overboard and sometimes the ultimate victim will drive people to consider that option. Why the 'Victim' is so powerful is that the sob story draws attention, people provide sympathy and care. When you work on a ship you have to pretend you care (I know that is harsh but knowing about Albert's haemorrhoids and the fact he can only sit for a maximum of twenty minutes isn't something I would choose to care about). In truth you are thinking about the next port and the next exciting thing you are going to do, completely zone out and nod at the appropriate moments. Why else would anyone work on a ship?

Essentially, many of the 'Victims' like a good moan or to share the intricate details of an illness so that they draw sympathy. Oh and please excuse me if I seem uncaring; however, when you have spent twenty-four hours a day, seven days a week for over a hundred and fifty days in a row without a day off (here is my 'Victim' turning up – yes I chose to do that) your tolerance levels diminish and you really couldn't give a flying crap about whether someone's wart got infected, especially during a five course meal. So back to the woeing war at the Officer's table. When you are at the end of your contract and you are counting down the hours and not the days, sometimes

144

the capacity to hold back becomes limited. In your mind you are dragging yourself towards the finish line and then you hear about Larry's swollen prostate over a Hogmanay haggis dinner. Honestly! So my advice to all those who wish to shut the 'Cruise Ship Creature Victim' up is to simply say 'Well this one guy I met got knob leprosy and his dick dropped off!' With that shake your head in sympathy mutter 'Poor Dereck,' and walk away. It works every time. People are stunned and are unable to react quickly enough. In no time the rumour will go around about a knob leper and it will soon evolve into the Captain having knob leprosy. That is what is so wonderful about confined spaces and general ship gossip or cruise whispers. You may wonder why this breed of 'Cruise Ship Creature' falls into the dangerous section. Well once you start to listen to them then they will seek you out and suck the life from you. It will be like they attach an emotional hoover to your ear and suck your brain out through it. Advice: figure out this kind of creature early on in the cruise and take small sausages everywhere you go and after delivering the knob leprosy line sneakily drop a little sausage on the floor and say 'Goodness – it looks like knob leprosy has already reached the ship'.

# CHAPTER 78

## THE SHIP'S PSYCHO

There are often mad people on their holidays, they are a little more than eccentric but every now and again the ultimate nutter manages to sneak up the gangway. There will be odd behaviours taking place all around the ship. He or she will turn up and do random things. How about playing a bugle on the front deck. Why would anyone try roller skating along the promenade deck during a storm? What about wearing arm bands in the Jacuzzi or using forks to launch peas at fellow passengers? My favourite was the snorkel wearer who stood for an hour in the on-deck shower by the pool. The guests side-ways glanced the strange sight until one of the crew ventured over to the shower and asked the shower snorkeler whether everything was okay. He was fine, very fine indeed.

The female version of 'The Ship's Psycho' often creates huge dramas and screams when she does not get her way. Tantrum in the atrium anyone? Ever seen a woman in her late fifties laying on the floor hitting it with all her might because she has not got a seat at the Captain's table? It is amazing what people will do to try and get their way.

One of the most concerning ship's nutters was the one who wore an Officer's uniform and strolled around the crew area. He was only fully found out when he was discovered trying to visit the engine room wearing whites - the tropical uniform, when most people would wear khakis or overalls. An additional give away was that his uniform was not quite ship's uniform. Obviously that begs the question what was his intention? When he was questioned he said that he was simply curious and no one ever asks an Officer what they are up to. Maybe he is right but clearly he has never worked on board a ship because wherever I went people were always asking me what I was up to and the name of the island that was on the horizon. 'Mystery Island' was a good answer to deliver before legging it to a hidden doorway.

Back to the Officer impersonator. Since there was a constant change over of Officers, due to contracts, no one ever really knew who anyone else was. This blighter even found his way to the Officer's wardroom and had a drink there. No one wanted to ask him who he was because he had cleverly selected a four stripe epaulette which meant that potentially he was quite high up the pecking order. It was like the 'King's New Clothes,' no one wanted to point out the obvious because they did not want to look stupid. What made him all the more authentic was that he even had a name badge too. He might have been able to continue undetected but he gave himself away by the engine visit slip up. Obviously this chap was disembarked but his reason for his strange ways was because he was curious about the behind the scenes life of the crew and had always wanted to be an Officer. I guess he was trying to fake it to make it.

# CHAPTER 79

## THE ENTITLED

One of the biggest challenges on board is dealing with those people who feel they are entitled or more deserving than others. The 'Entitled' have mastered the craft of providing reason why they deserve more. They will use how many days they have cruised with the company or how much money they spent on the cruise to initiate the entitlement monologue. Once they have the 'Entitled' engagement then all their manipulative reasons will be justified with all kinds of evidence. You may wonder what I am talking about; however, one guest went for the 'I am entitled to an upgrade' by bringing a dead mouse on to the ship. Imagine actually bringing a dead mouse onto the ship as evidence. The reason that we know that the deceased creature was not from the ship is because we asked to have the mouse as evidence and then sent it for a mouse post-mortem which placed the time of mouse death one week prior to the ship's departure. Of course it could have died on the ship a week before; however, the post-mortem provided other insights that made it clear that the guest had used a mouse that its cat had hunted as a reason for an upgrade.

Two pairs of soiled underwear found in life-jackets was one of the more random entitlement excuses. One of the guests slammed two pairs of dirty soiled underwear on the reception desk and demanded he and his wife be given a penthouse for the disgust he felt at discovering such items in the lifejackets. That one was quite a challenge because how do you prove that the dirty knickers don't actually belong to the guest concerned?

What is particularly bemusing are the guests who intend to take part in a world voyage and spend time plotting, planning and preparing how they are going to get money back or seek compensation. Why don't you just enjoy the cruise rather than find ways to justify entitlement and get money back?

You may wonder why the 'Entitled' have been added to the dangerous list. Well infectious entitlement is a contagious. As soon as one 'Entitled' declares why they are so entitled then the next thing you know someone else is declaring their reason for being entitled. In a short time, there is an entitlement-demic where everyone is entitled beyond belief. These 'Cruise Ship Creatures' also straddle the 'Out Woers' and the 'Do You Know Who I Ams?'

# CHAPTER 80

## THE DIRTY OLD MEN AND THE EQUALLY DODGY WOMEN

In general the 'Cougars' (older women hunting for a younger man) are a little bit glamorous and have something a little 'sexy' about them. They radiate a certain confidence and they are generally attractive. At the other end of the scale we have the 'Dirty Old Men'. Some of them are excited by female Officers. They purposely stalk them and make lude comments to any woman with brocade. 'Ooooh Officer, I like the white uniform because you can practically see through it.' Unfortunately, you can't slap a guest but you can report them. One chap from a Penthouse thought it was perfectly okay to stroke female crew's bottoms when they bent over (for example when cleaning). He was very wealthy and assumed he could get away with it. When he was reported to the Captain, the Captain called him in and advised the chap that if he made any further approaches he would be disembarked in the next port. The next port was Djibouti, a port that you do not want to be banished to.

Other 'Dirty Old Men' chase anything, especially knowing that some nationalities are so polite they will accept the harassment. Then there are the flashers. Yep... the flasher mac on deck with boots and socks was quite a phenomenon. At certain twilight hours he would jump out wearing socks, brown boots, a flasher mac and peak hat. Admittedly he did wear a red and white sock over the offending droopy appendage. He was in his late seventies with white hair and it made him quite a challenge to identify because that description applied to the majority of the male guests on the ship. Imagine having to attend an identity parade with that one. He was the Security Officer's nightmare because he would flash and go. He seemed to know the quickest escape routes too. He turned up on the surveillance cameras, would pop into the loo and wait for other potential looky-likeys to go inside. He was good, he was practiced and he was caught. Who would have thought a red and white stripy knob sock would give him away? The cabin steward noticed the offending sock and advised Security. They then watched his comings and flashing goings. The chap was caught and taken to the Captain to discuss his flashy misdemeanours. He had no remorse, instead he said that quite often, at certain times of the day, he got warm and needed to cool down. The way he did that was open his jacket. Everyone can justify behaviour even the ship's flasher.

## CHAPTER 81

## THE RUDE AND THE ANGRY RED FACE

I am not going to spend an enormous amount of time on this 'Cruise Ship Creature' because they are quite apparent around the reception desk on embarkation day or before disembarkation when it comes to paying bills. In fact, you may well see one of the 'Rude and The Angry Red Face' brigade even before you embark. They are often hanging around the car drop-off point having a bit of a meltdown. When they are in a couple they refer to each other as DARLING! As though they are shouting the affectionate term with venom. They then make their way into the embarkation hall and it is then that the couple unite. All the while they rile each other up and have to direct their anger elsewhere. As soon as they find their victim to unleash their emotional vomit, they calm down. I noticed this 'Cruise Ship Creature' very early on in my cruising career. I actually learned to spot them at a long distance and make myself scarce. The problem was that the angry are like atoms and their shaking angry behaviour causes others to become angry until you have a mob of 'Angry Red Faces'. I have to say this type of 'Cruise Ship Creature' was a blessing to me because I learned the art of stopping them mid-flow. This is for those who might be a little adventurous and fancy trying out a couple of techniques to remain unaffected by them. So as they unleash, most people will sit quietly and listen. When I first started learning how to deal with them I would gaze at a point in the middle of their forehead. Psychologically that put me in a power position. Try it. I would let them go on and on ranting and ranting while I didn't take it in. When they were finally finished I asked what they thought the solution was. After a time, I came to the conclusion that I was not interested in being an anger sponge. There were a lot of angry people in the cruising world. It seemed that every cruise there would be a fresh influx, so I had to learn a way of self-protection. Potentially there were a lot of hours dealing with people's anger issues. I came to the conclusion that life could be spent doing far better things like smiling and having nice conversations. So when they began the rant I would say 'STOP, how do we put this into two sentences?' That would divert their thought and generally break the angry spiel. Finally, I just came to the conclusion that it was better to spot the angry person and decide not to engage. That was when I recognised the fact that there were a whole breed of 'Angry Red-Faced' 'Cruise Ship Creatures' who no matter what you did for them they still couldn't help being angry. The simplest thing would trigger them into an anger detonation. In terms of spotting them, it is best to be aware of the creature and simply avoid being around them. Anger is contagious and so is plague.

## THE DEALS... WE GET CRUISE DEALS... WE BET OUR DEAL IS BETTER THAN YOURS

'Everyone loves a deal,' apparently. Then there are those who love a deal so much that when they get it then they have to tell everyone how cheap their cruise deal was. No doubt you have heard those really annoying cruisers who love to let everyone know how much they paid for their cruise. 'Oh it was such a bargain that we could hardly resist could we darling? We weren't even planning to go on holiday but we just couldn't miss out,' they enthuse. Or 'Oh it was just such a wonderful price. We couldn't believe it... We booked last minute and got the cruise for a ridiculous price. In fact when we think about it, the company are practically paying us to be here.' They then reference all the other really cheap deals they have managed to get over the years and really aggravate the other passengers.

When the 'Mr and Mrs We Get Cruise Deals,' join a table in the restaurant they can't help but launch into that very same conversation with a malicious smirk. It seems that not only do they love smugly aggravating everyone in near vicinity, they also like to talk very loudly about how cheap their deal was so that the whole restaurant can hear them.

This type of 'Cruise Ship Creature' often becomes addicted to the deals and evolve into serial cheap-cruise addicts who are constantly on the hunt for cheap deals. The thing is, and for those who paid a fair price, you might want to know that those who get the deals usually get the rubbish cabins with the noise. Yes, people can get bargains but what they don't know is that those bargains are there for a reason. On a ship you have different cabin types. The better quality cabins usually go first. The discounted cabins are usually those that have had the most complaints or have had to be refitted or something changed. For example, one of the cheap cabins had a pipe behind the wardrobe that leaked into it and made the cabin smell damp. Did the person who got the extreme bargain know that before they sailed? What about the cabin that suffers constant toilet blockages? Oh maybe that one was sold off cheap too. What about the creaky cabin that as soon as the ship hits any wave bigger than a metre sounds as though there are woodpeckers in the walls? My favourite cheapy moment was the last minute deal on the cabin that had recently had an infestation of bed bugs. When someone gets something cheap there is usually a reason for it. So this wonderful 'Cruise Ship Creature', may well have found a deal but maybe they wouldn't be quite so braggy if they knew why that particular cabin happened to be that much cheaper than the others. In addition many of the cheap cabins are located in areas of vibration or are placed next to the morgue. With that in mind, the next time you meet 'Mr and Mrs Cruise Deals', you can happily smile to yourself knowing that they probably are lying beside where dead bodies are stored or where sewage leaked through a wardrobe.

How to spot these creatures: if a conversation starts with 'So how much did you pay for your cruise?' then it is worth using the 'escape word' and leave the conversation as soon as possible unless you have a better bargain than them. What you will notice about this type is they will wait until everyone has shared how much they paid and then say something sizeably less. Bear in mind they may also be compulsive liars. My advice is don't get involved, don't engage and don't play their game.

## CHAPTER 83

## THE 'CAN I ASK A STUPID QUESTION?'

'Can I ask a stupid question?' Why would you ask that question when you know it is a stupid question? In fact, you have already exceeded your stupid question quota by knowing it is a stupid question and asking it. Of course on the ship the reply is 'There is no such thing as a stupid question.' Unfortunately, my reply was 'If you think it is stupid then why would you ask it?' The response was an expression of bemusement combined with trapped wind. Of course the stupid questioner continued because once that stupid question has arisen into consciousness then it has to be asked or justified. What makes it worse is that unless that stupid question is released the originator will be endlessly tortured until the stupid answer is provided. So what was the stupid question? Oh it was an epic: 'If there are sperm whales are there also egg whales?' My answer – 'Yes'. I then walked off completely unaware of the repercussions of being a git. I know what you are thinking 'What a bitch!' Well actually I found it hilarious especially when that same passenger announced to other passengers that not only were there sperm whales there were also egg whales. She then said that one of the Officers had confirmed her eggy whale suspicions. Well the 'Launderette Gossips' generated my karma and told the whole ship that one of the female Officers had advised a passenger that egg whales existed. Of course with the help of the cruise ship whispers the egg whale comment gained momentum and evolved into a Moby Eggy Dick saga. Quite clearly egg whales were larger than the sperm whale and there were less of them. When a sperm whale was aware of an egg whale it swam at great speed and butted it until pregnancy ensued. The story that developed from one comment was phenomenal. It is with such occasions you realise that you should never mess with the 'Launderette Gossips' and consider answering stupid questions in an intelligent way.

NOTE: You might wonder why the 'Can I Ask A Stupid Question?' have fallen into the 'Dangerous' breed. Well if you allow one stupid question then you will fall into a deluge of questions verging on ridiculous. When word goes around that you answer stupid questions you may well be hunted down by all of those 'Stupid Question Creatures' to be tormented with a deluge of general stupidity. This could be a very dangerous situation!

## CHAPTER 84

## THE 'I MUST HAVE THE FRONT SEAT OF THE BUS!'

What is it about the front seat of a bus? Yes, you can see a bit more but why do people fight for that front position? I have watched guests argue over that seat and then attempt to pull each other off the seat. When a tour is called in the theatre 'The I Must Have A Front Seat' gang dart down to the gangway at the fastest pace you can ever imagine. Often miracle of healing takes place when an invalid spots the potential position of bussing viewerage power! They then get to the bus and feign a limp, produce a walking stick or demand the front seat based on an invented disease. Often the seats are reserved for those less mobile. It when eight people compete against each other to justifying why they suffer more pain than the others to get the front seat of the bus. The reasons spiral into absurdity where people pluck out false eyes and wave them – that is when you know the world has gone mad. In hindsight it might be worth designing a very wide bus with only front seats to stop bus front seat conflict.

The other type of front seat demanders are those who wait for the ship to be cleared by authorities and get out to the car park before the buses are set up. As soon as the bus is free they are there. They have nabbed the front seat.

Another little trick they pull is when the buses are being loaded, the sneak off like Ninjas to the next bus before the previous bus is full. This backfired when a certain couple thought they were being clever, snuck onto the next bus and missed their tour. Instead they climbed onto the free shuttle bus. Since they had been so determined, the driver let them sit there. Woops! Never mind.

Many of the 'I Must Have The Front Seat' have developed their techniques over time. They know that people don't like confrontation, so if the worst comes to the worst they will shout, scream and pull actual tantrums. Watching a woman wearing a visor lying face down in a carpark pummelling the floor to get a front seat is a spectacle worth beholding. Obviously standing with a huge grin on my face did not ingratiate myself to her. When you are at the end of a contract then nothing phases you. So I left the woman pummelling the floor until I loaded the bus and then advised her that there was one seat left at the back. This resulted in tears, stamping and general outrage. 'I can refund you if you don't want the seat,' I said without emotion. Her jaw dropped. All her tried and tested tactics had failed. 'You can get a taxi and go yourself. It will cost you four times the amount of the tour. The choice is yours. I have two minutes until I have to send the bus.' Oh the satisfaction... Of course she got on the bus. When people threaten you with their walking stick that is a different matter. You would have thought that this couple went round duelling with walking sticks as a profession. (Remember the previous 'Walking Stick Dueller' creature?) They were the type of angry old people that were bent over and looked as though they had spent the last fifty years sucking a lemon. When it came to the front seat demands, the old chap began to shout. That is standard; however, when they swear you know it isn't going to end well. Finally, he intimidated the tour staff and when he did not get his way lifted his walking stick aggressively. He demanded a front seat and a personal onslaught ensued accusing the tour staff of not being accommodating. It is always good to record these little attacks on your phone and then send in the Security staff to abate the threatening behaviour. Unfortunately, that old couple did not make it to Miraculous Fatima for the healing because Security extracted them from the situation. They then created more commotion so were disembarked the next day. Goodbye.

# CHAPTER 85

## THE OUT WOERS – WOE WOE AND MORE BOLLOCKY WOE...

So we may as well get the more negative sorts lumped together and over and done with. So... the 'I Must Have The Front Seat On The Bus,' often straddle into another category along with the 'Victim'. You see I have witnessed a 'woe off' yes it is a thing. When people want the front seat of a bus they will come up with all manner of story to get it. So you will hear – 'Well I have had a hip operation.' 'Well I have had a hip and knee operation.' 'Well I have had open heart surgery, two hips replaced and a knee, so I deserve the front seat.' Then there was the side winder 'I have had three hips replaced, two knees, I am missing a bollock and I can't smell anything.' 'Do you need me to ask reception if any bollocks have been handed in to lost and found?' said with a very straight face, at the perfect moment. 'I lost three bollocks... They weren't handed in.' So what do you do with that? Obviously there is compulsive lying and a hint of exaggeration, when people want something they will say whatever they can to get what they want. Oh and I may have exaggerated the story with the three bollocks; although it is amazing what comes from people's mouths when they intend to win.

On formal nights, Officers were expected to waft around and socialise. During these spangley dress-to-impress events it is best to purposely avoid clusters of people discussing ailments. Wouldn't you rather have fun? My reason for avoidance is that my capacity for delivering a completely inappropriate line at a defining moment is now second to none. One can usually get away with it if the line is said in a jovial tone and a smile finishes the sentence. Although, as mentioned in the plastic surgery section, I have been privy to some very interesting conversations about plastic surgery and who has had what done and how much they had spent on it. When people have a spare one hundred and twenty grand to inflate their bosoms and be 'reformed' I hide my absolute shock by thinking about giant tortoises eating ripe bananas. It really can alter your facial expression from 'You have to be joking,' to 'Oh bloody hell,' with a hint of concern.

## CHAPTER 86

## THE 'I USED TO WORK ON A SHIP'

There are know it alls and there are ship know it alls. I probably fall into this category now because when I go on holiday on a cruise I have secret knowledge of what goes on behind the scenes and the kind of things that the crew say about the guests. I purposely keep my cruise ship working history quiet because in all honesty it is quite annoying when someone announces in a loud voice 'I know how this works because I used to work on ships.'

There are of course the other 'I Used To Work On A Ship' type. They loved working on ships and retired and have returned for a cruise just to be in the cruisey world once more. They desperately want to be involved or feel a deep sense of nostalgia about being on a cruise ship. The problem is that if something goes wrong due to weather conditions, or changes in itineraries etc, these 'I Used To Work On A Ship' can be the bane of Officers' lives because often this type of creature gravitate to each other (as if a strange magnetic field draws them in) and they attempt to figure out what has gone on. There have been times when this creature has caused uprisings based on their previous ship knowledge, which unfortunately was incorrect because they were not aware of the full series of events that had taken place behind the scenes. The truth is when you have worked on a ship, you generally have great memories of your time on board and adventures you have experienced... that is after time has passed and true exhaustion has waned. The only problem is that when a ship gets into difficulties and guests need to go to muster stations – the biggest hindrance and the biggest danger is the 'I Have Worked On A Ship' type because they will undermine the crew who have been trained in evacuation. What you may well be surprised to learn is that there is essentially a 'naughty corner or place' for those who are 'disruptive in emergency situation' people. If they create uproar they are taken to 'the naughty person location' in an emergency so that they do not mess up evacuations or create panic. So if you are an 'I Used To Work On A Ship' type then I suggest that in an emergency you keep your shippy experience to yourself.

## PART 8

## THE REBELLIOUS CRUISE SHIP CREATURES

You will soon learn there are rebels with a cruise ship cause. This breed like to go against the rules or test the rule boundaries. Yet the irony is that the whole shippy environment is based on rules. Some of the cruisey characters listed here are rebellious by nature and others are rebellious by choice. Enjoy this group because they are the ones who lead uprisings and mutinies.

## CHAPTER 87

## THE SMOKERS CORNER

Smoking can cause quite an issue on the ships because if a lit cigarette is tossed over the side it can be picked up by the wind and land in random places and start fires. This is quite a well-known issue and the crew repeatedly have the message drummed into them. There are those guests that simply can't go without a cigarette and will brave the most challenging conditions, usually wearing pyjamas and a dressing gown, so they can get that nicotine fix. When I have been doing my Officer's rounds, I have been dressed in special wet weather gear and circumnavigated the decks at six in the morning to find clusters of smokers gathered in sheltered areas on the deck puffing away. There also seemed to be certain timings when they would all gather. It could be minus ten on a northern lights cruise, it would be dark and freezing outside but there would still be a plume of cigarette smoke. Obviously there are those who attempt to sneak a cigarette in their cabin; however, if a cabin steward discovers a smoking incident then they have to report it. Can you imagine being disembarked from a cruise ship because you snuck a ciggy in the toilet? It has happened. There are rules on ships and if the passengers and crew are put in danger then goodbye!

Other than that, it is amazing how many smokers are found on deck wearing their nighties in the Caribbean. I often went running at 5.00am or 5.30am (depending on when I started duty) and there they were: half asleep with a lit cigarette hanging from their lip. There wouldn't just be one smoker in that state either. The group would be gathered with bed hair, half-asleepness and that first cigarette to start the day. The nighty thing was also a bit of a concern because they billow. In fact, a nighty and a cigarette were technically a health and safety issue. Imagine a situation where it is windy, there is a cigarette and the billowy nighty is lifted at an inconvenient angle at a specific moment and makes contact with the lit cigarette. Not only is the potential for a fire but also the potential to be emotionally scarred by witnessing what is lurking beneath that cotton beauty when the wind lifts it for unsuspecting onlookers.

# CHAPTER 88

## THE LAUNDERETTE GOSSIPS

Gossips naturally gravitate to gossips and the best place on the ship to discover gossip or be fed complete and utter drivel is in the launderette. Some guests have even advised me that they go and make up a story, sit in the launderette and then share it. Sometimes they are not even doing their washing. One of my favourite rumours that went around the ship, which originated in the launderette, was that on the world cruise there were eleven bodies in the morgue. It was not true, but it amused me when I was asked. 'So… we hear there are eleven bodies in the morgue…'

'That's interesting…' I replied with a smirk.

'Why is that interesting?' asked one of the gossips with a curious tone.

'Well the morgue can only hold three bodies.'

'Oh,' she replied thoughtfully.

'It couldn't even reach that capacity if they were top to tail. Of course they wouldn't do that anyway. They would have to find somewhere else to keep them.' When that popped out of my mouth I knew that only gossipy doom could ensue. A twinkle appeared in the gossip's eyes. She had questions and she was also immersed in gossipacious creativity. That was my cue to depart with a sense of urgency. 'Just got to go and feed the Captain's cat!'

Well the gossip certainly became more interesting. The gossips, with five more days at sea, had plenty of time to mischief monger. They had to justify their eleven body claims. So apparently there was now an allocated cabin for bodies. There were a couple of bodies in the brig. In fact, the ship had run out of space for bodies – according to the gossips. The next thing would be body buddies, where you might wake up in the night with a body laid out next to you. Oh and according to the gossips the body count after seven days at sea had reached thirteen. The truth was there were actually two in total and during the voyage we had a heli-evacuation, where a person was air-lifted off the ship for a medical emergency. Of course the rumour then became that we ran out of space for the dead bodies and now they were having to airlift them away or throw them overboard.

The rumour expanded further, not only did the morgue have eleven bodies stuffed inside, the other options could not take any additional dead people, the only place left were fridges. The fridges were going to be cleared for anyone else who planned on departing the world (according to the gossip). I just want to point out this is completely untrue and the gossips certainly manufacture some incredibly tall shippy tales!

One more thing about the 'Launderette Gossips' ... as much as they are brilliant, they sometimes turf things up that have an element of truth. For example, one of the engines was broken and it was likely that we were going to miss a port. The gossips figured it out even before the crew knew about the situation.

Another time the gossips noticed a series of affairs taking place. The reality is on ships the crew don't bat an eyelid at the transient nature of relationships that take place. Yet a keen eyed gossipy observer entered the launderette with something that would certainly cause a sea-day-stir. The gossip spread like wild engine fire and the super-sausagey culprit was confronted by his wife who had just arrived on board, the girlfriend, the three guests that he was 'keeping warm' and his boyfriend. Quite an extreme gossip resolution.

Honestly the things that the guests come up with have me in hysterics. They often create back stories for Officers and crew who are completely unaware of their freshly created torrid history that resulted in them being at sea. According to the shippy gossips we are all running away. I like that concept - the strange thing is that on ship you can't actually run anywhere. It is more of a luxury prison than a luxury escape. Think about it – you work seventy hours a week and you have to be nice to people whether you like them or not. You are on the ship a minimum of four months and you can't leave unless you can get past Security (we swipe out). Abseiling would be a challenge and stealing a lifeboat might be a little tricky. The ship holds the crews' passports and you can't do what you want when you want. Where is the running away in that little set up?

## CHAPTER 89

## THE HYSTERICAL LAUGHERS

There are so many different types of laugh; doesn't that make laughing fantastic? As we all know there is nothing better than a good belly laugh until you can't breathe. Tears run down your cheeks and your stomach feels as though you have done two thousand sit ups. So why is it that on a ship, when someone laughs in a confined space regularly, especially in the restaurant, that people roll their eyes or grow aggravated?

There were times when I have hosted tables where the guests have been in a complete state of laughter lunacy; shrill laughs mixed with witchy cackles accompanied by guttural chortles. My favourite was the laugh that sounded as though it was going to hit the peak note in an opera. Imagine if all the glasses smashed... The combined harmony amongst the gigglaceous group resembled an out of tune orchestra teamed with a hyena. I loved it and so did they. Tears cascaded down their cheeks as they fought to catch their breath. It was just lovely yet there were disgusted looks from the boring tables surrounding us. I felt for those Officers who had been given the 'I have a dank smell lurking under my nose' brigade to host.

Have you noticed that when people are being looked at by people who are not impressed by their laughter it makes them laugh more? Oh and my table laughed, so much so they were shaking and unable to eat. It was awesome. The trigger was a simple discovery that one of the guys had accidentally sleep-walked naked on the ship. All the implications of what could happen played through our minds. We discussed where his route took him and whether he wore a Captain's hat on the journey. The thing was this group were happy, positively infectious and everything created the opportunity for a good hearty giggle. During the rest of the cruise I ran into this lovely group and they attracted other fun people to them while the miseries and the complainers glared at them. Whenever there was raucous laughter there was a sneer. Now imagine one of the complainers actually

169

made a full complaint to the Captain about the fact that a certain group of disruptive laughers were purposely ruining other people's cruises by adopting unnecessary laughter! Oh yes. So what did the Captain do? He advised the guest to join in the fun because that was what cruising was about. Needless to say there were further complaints about the Captain condoning excessive laughter in public areas. With that in mind, enjoy laughing hysterically.

# CHAPTER 90

## THE COUGARS

These ladies have been hinted at previously; although I feel they need some proper focus. There are older women who like to prowl the decks for a younger man. In fact, it is not just the decks: it is the corridors and the bars. Some are after Officers and others are after… well anyone as long as they are younger than them. Women in their seventies desire chaps in their forties and women in their fifties prowl amongst the thirty year olds. It is a fascinating dynamic. Often the 'Cougars' travel in pairs and stalk with a specific young man strategy. In the evening the waiters are subject to suggestion and many a bar man is asked for an alternative sausage cocktail. There are women who even lull crew into their cabin by reporting a noise, a leak or an issue. They are often suggestively dressed and leave nothing to the imagination. There is generally a lot of bending down and lip licking, not their own lips either. Some of the 'Cougars' even pounce on unsuspecting crew or ask them for assistance which involves some interesting positioning that might emulate dogs reproducing. Some of the 'Cougars' are fantastic, with young figures, beautiful clothing and perfumes that overpower. Although there are others who should have been put out to pasture and have told me they are past their sell-by date and are cougaring above their station. They admit they love the challenge. When I have engaged in conversations with them they have been open and honest about their escapades and asked who of the younger crew was more open to suggestion. When I responded, 'It isn't worth the crew member's job' they smiled with a twinkle in their eye and stated that they may as well give it a go… I am often amazed by how many achieve their goal when a flushed cabin steward emerges from a cabin with a glow in his cheeks that can only reveal one thing: the air-conditioning is at fault and the toilet needed a bloody good scrub!

# CHAPTER 91

## THE REBEL WITH A BUDGIE SMUGGLING CAUSE

This particular creature includes those who are the budgie smugglers of doom, sand in sock spectaculars and salami rustlers.

Budgie smuggling should be outlawed. It just isn't right to smuggle a budgie in a pair of skimpy speedo swimming trunks. Oh that isn't actually a budgie? When you are talking budgie smuggling you mean that there isn't actually a small squashed bird being transported against its will in a Lycra arrangement that surrounds a man's thrustacious hip girdle? Oh instead there is a male sausage budgie imposter being smuggled in a pair of Lycra trunks... Nice! Surely those disturbing items of clothing should be renamed sausage smugglers or salami smugglers... Actually thinking about it, the term budgie smugglers reached the mass, I wonder how many people noticed that many of the budgies being smuggled did not actually have beaks.

Now that we have the above clear, there is many a disturbing sight to be witnessed around the pool. Salamis of all shapes and sizes are smuggled, squashed and flaunted. At times you wonder whether the Borat thong has accidentally been applied because the trunks are so small and the wearer is soooooooooooooooooo big. One of my Australian friends referred to one particularly offensive sight: 'He looks like all he is wearing is a dick sticker.' A South African friend recoiled when a chap bent over and cried 'It looks like wet sand in a sock.' All of these observations based on the simplicity of a pair of trunks, a bit of sunshine and the dream of getting some decisive tan lines!

# CHAPTER 92

## THE 'I HAVE 20 SUITCASES'

Do you have a suitcase madam? The general response from an embarking guest is to point at one or two suitcases but in some instances people have packed for all eventuality and have at least ten suitcases, for only one week. Ultimately the 'I Have 20 Suitcases' is rebelling against minimalistic packing. One of the other 'Cruise Ship Creatures' is the 'Dress-tastic' and she often has a plethora of well-stuffed suitcases containing a dress for every occasion and more. Admittedly some of the cruisy chaps are equally as packing-prolific and bring all manner of formal wear, strangely ornate suits, tweedy little numbers, an abundance of bow ties, safari wear, a Captain's hat and more socks to be paired with sandals than you could ever envision. Just consider a multitude of shades of beige socks to be sandal-ised in the sunshine. I just need to deviate, what happens with tan lines regarding these chaps who have socks that cut off half way up their calves? It is not as if you can stop the socky offender, shove your finger in their calf-high-sock and take a peek to see if there is a major difference between sock-covered skin and leggily exposed skin. There have been some fantastic accidental bandana tan lines where a sharp dividing line cuts across the middle of a forehead. In an attempt to balance this tan-line travesty out, red lipstick was massaged into the unexposed area. Obviously the bandana incident was accidental but these chaps purposely wear long socks in the sun. Maybe they do it so that when they go to bed or meet a new woman they can convince themselves they are still wearing socks in bed even if they are just tan lines... This could be one of humanities greatest sockily-clad conundrums.

Back to the mass suitcase onslaught... It is understandable when the 'World Cruisers' join the ship they may have more suitcases than most. They could be on board for around 110 -120 days and that means a lot of underwear or maybe no underwear at all. Now if you don't want to do washing then you will need a lot of clothes or actually pay the laundry to do your washing. Alternatively, you can join the 'Launderette Gossips' for a washing with gossip session and discover all the invented stories from around the ship. People do love to dress up on a cruise and that means loads-a-luggage. What is even more amusing is when the 'World Cruisers' disembark, many have purchased items from all around the world. Imagine 'stuff' from at least thirty ports! Quite often their luggage doubles. So much so on some ships there is a luggage delivery service because it is often impossible to fit it all that new stuff in a car, a coach or a train. Imagine after loading up the car with luggage turning to your partner, 'Erm sorry darling there isn't enough room for you – you will have to walk.'

PART 9


THE FOODY OR LIQUID LOVING CRUISE SHIP CREATURES

There is no denying that going on a luxury cruise provides the opportunity to stuff your face twenty-four hours a day. So many people take cruises simply to eat, snack, gobble, wolf, munch and excessively masticate in public. It is an acceptable cruise pastime. Of course there are others who prefer to 'dine' and frequent the more exclusive restaurants. With exclusivity certain foody creatures materialise. We have many a different consuming creature who may also be teamed with the liquid loving beast. Here is a whole section dedicated to gorging, glugging, chomping and swigging.


CHAPTER 93

THE BUFFET BANDITS


What makes cruising so appealing is the fact that there is food available twenty-four hours per day. There is early breakfast, late breakfast, brunch, lunch, afternoon tea, dinner, late night buffet, room service, midnight buffet and more room service. The ship is a glutton's dream and a dieter's nightmare. With that constant flow of food, how do you think most people respond? Erm... stuff their face! In all honesty I have never known anything like it. It really is fascinating watching people pile up their plates and create food mountains of a monumental scale. At first I was bemused by it because I could not understand why people would want to eat so much, so of course I had to ask the question. You might think it is rude to ask why someone is eating so much, well some guests believe it is their right to ask you everything about your life – so why not do the same? So the question was tailored in an inoffensive way 'Well you clearly like the food here... Is there a reason you visited the buffet five times? ' woops. 'Yep, the more we eat the more we get our money's worth.' Ahhhh 'Eat more to get your money's worth.' It was a strange concept, that by stuffing one's face, a person had their money's worth on the cruise. People piled up three or four plates of food and they devoured it all. I had mistakenly assumed they simply wanted to try as many different foods as possible - like a taster dinner. Nope, I was very wrong. It was all down to volume.

After that simple interaction I became curious and began to track and trend the face stuffers. Some might call it stuffer stalking, it wasn't because I simply watched how the buffet worked. I could take my editing to a table and watch and write notes. So it seemed there were a number of approaches to the buffet. On the embarkation day of the cruise, the guests were still in a 'figure it out' phase, where they were still accustomed to the portions they had at home. Also the buffet was guestily disorganised with no real lining up. A systemised approach had not yet developed; instead it was a bit of a foody-free-for-all. On the first morning (usually a day at sea) there was generally a late surge of guests because most people had decided to lie in. That was when all kind of sneaky buffet antics took place. There were people who worked in teams to distract others to get in line. There were people creeping ahead of others to have an omelette made. Poached egg demands became ridiculous and there was actual poaching of pre-ordered poached eggs. I wonder if that is why they were called poached originally. Someone knew that an egg was going to be thieved by others. In the meantime, there were even those who threw yoghurts across the room to be caught by another when the stock became limited. It was nuts. Talking about nuts, have you ever witnessed someone playing with their nuts? There was one chap who liked to arrange the walnuts in a line. It seemed he thought they looked like little brains. Honestly, some of the randomness of the ship simply amazes me.

As the cruise wore on guests increased their initial volumes so that they did not have to return to the buffet to re-stock. You would have thought that people were storing up for a long hard winter when the

176

reality was they simply had two days at sea until they reached Madeira or some other lovely destination.

So consider the following behaviour seemed to be the triggers and it soon became apparent that as soon as the sanitiser was applied to the hands that the guests switched into buffet-bandit mode. It was the same as the conditioning for boxers when the bell sounded to start a round. The sanitiser squirt made a 'ding' in their minds which resulted in some of the most random behaviour: a sprint to get a tray and out of focus eyes as food was piled at a rate without thought. When the bandits met a buffet-road-block they would study the other passengers' plates for potential snack-swipage. There were even times when rolls were abducted from an unsuspecting party's plate. It was phenomenal. That was just the evening buffet. As I mentioned earlier the mass of guests moved in swathes. So port days became increasingly exciting. Since there were tours to take, the mass had to eat early and be ready. In addition, being off the ship meant that rather than buy food ashore, ship food would be smuggled by the guests. My goodness not being able to eat for at least two hours took a psychological toll. So there we are at the early morning buffet and all manner of bag and serviette was filled with rolls, muffins, fruit and croissants. My personal favourite was watching people hide bananas in their pockets. 'Is that a banana in your pocket sir or are you just pleased to see me?'

'Erm no I am going on tour.' It seemed that bananas were the choice of the glorious guesties. So banana smuggling aside, the increased surge of buffets guests pre-tour was fascinating, the smuggling was a phenomenon and... the outcry when in certain countries passengers were not allowed to take food ashore. Oh the handing in of smuggled food was delightful to observe.

Imagine this: we had a thousand people in a theatre who were waiting to go on a tour in New Zealand and as part of the agricultural legalities people are not allowed to take food ashore. First of all imagine the uproar. It was amazing how everyone wanted to justify the banana in their pocket. People were threatened with a huge fine and potential imprisonment because of a smuggled sausage or banana. The authorities even brought on sniffer dogs... It was that serious. So the announcement went out asking everyone to give up their food and place it on the theatre stage otherwise they could be arrested. Well a moment later the stage looked like a harvest festival. It seemed the whole buffet made a sudden resurrection on stage. There were bacon butties, every fruit you could imagine and... more bananas that you could shake a walking stick at. With a thousand people in the room, it seemed that at least fifty percent had banana smuggled. In such situations the 'Entitled' come into their own. Imagine the stories and justifications made by the 'Entitled' as to why they should be allowed to break the country's law and take that banana ashore!

So you have an idea about pre-tours, well after the guests have been on tour what do you think they do? Maybe they pop into the local town and dine at a local restaurant? Oh no. Why would they do that? They wouldn't be getting their money's worth. Why pay when all that food is sitting there waiting? On a port day the prime hours between twelve and two reveals queues of people stampeding up the gangway to the lunch buffet. The swarm descend like locusts and devour everything in their sight. Plates are piled to the ceiling and everything goes. Elbow jabs, distraction techniques and general arguments have unfolded next to the cold meat section. Salads are usually less stressful yet the meat and seafood areas carry a higher value when it comes to getting one's money's worth. A hint of lobster or steak can easily end in tears if the resupply does not happen fast enough.

Obviously there are other buffets throughout the day; however, the one that bemuses me the most is the midnight buffet. Why on earth does anyone need food at midnight? Well I found out the answer to that. It seems that after a bit of drinking and a bit of dancing in the disco the guests believe they have burned off a calorie which means they can definitely have some kind of tart as reward. When I mention tart I mean a dessert tart rather than the 'I've had a few drinks and I am everybody's kind of tart.' So when the clock strikes midnight you can witness a stampede to the cake-filled buffet. You might think that people would be more reserved at midnight but no... the plate piling continues and all manner of tart, cake and gateau are consumed. There are savoury options including meat on sticks and what appear to be samosas but the general midnight munching mayhem seems to revolve mostly around cake. Cake makes people happy and that is a fatty fact until they have to spend six months working off the fourteen pounds they gained in two weeks on their cruise. What I find amazing is that often guests bring on two sets of clothes. One set to arrive in and a second set to expand into and leave in. Amazing eh?

# CHAPTER 94

## THE WINE SNIFFERS

Showy, blowy and nasally glowy this connoisseur will loudly share their great insight into the world of wine. 'There is bouquet of wet dog combined with raspberries, a courgette and succulent aroma of string beans in this fine wine.' They swill the rouge liquid through their teeth like mouth wash and spit it into an available dish as though they are at the dentist. The captivated audience nods merrily as they shove their noses in the glass and do not want to admit that it smells a bit like fruity vinegar with a tang of cherry. The next wine is poured into another glass, the connoisseur cleans his palette, makes a huge show... and does some weird facial exercises that resemble someone playing an invisible trombone. Finally, with that look of absolute knowing and lip smacking he takes a sip, appears orgasmic as he traces the detail of the flavoursome liquid and... 'Alpaca anus combined with a woody window-wash and a hint of lavender. That lavender tickles the tastes buds and sends me into the Alpaca field to deliciously devour the tantalising and sumptuous... deeee....light.'

Looks of admiration fill the wine tasting event attendees. If only they had the capacity to identify an Alpaca's anus amongst the multitude of winey aromas and flavours. What a talent to be able to divulge such a sumptuous oral experience. Of course a connoisseur needs to practice, to identify and be convincing in the depth of wine sniffing and tasting mastery. What's more, their whiff-wording capacity is celebrated at such a tasting event; however, when one hosts a table and does not drink wine and asks someone to taste on the table's behalf then that is when the 'Wine Sniffer' takes whimsical wine worlds to a whole new level. Be warned you can be carried away with bizarre descriptions and random imagery as soon as the 'Wine Sniffer' inhales and shares insights that reveal an entirely random nasally experienced universe.

# CHAPTER 95

## THE COFFEE CONNOISSEURS

Some people just need a coffee in the morning, or the afternoon or through the day. There are those that love coffee and those who can't live without it. I always found it fascinating when doing my Officer duties at sunrise, which was known as doing the rounds, how so many people were actually up on deck hugging a coffee. They may well be in their dressing gown; they may have gravity-defying hair but they still had a coffee as they stared bleary eyed out to sea trying to work out where they were.

On numerous ships there were coffee lounges too where there were branded coffees to choose from. On the British ships there was a sudden influx of guests around ten thirty because that was when coffee suddenly had a cake to accompany it. The cake was paramount because cakes and cruising are a combination that enables the feeling of absolute joy. Never mind whether the guests had recently had a ten course breakfast, if there was quality coffee and cake to boot then they wanted it. Is it any wonder that guests have to be rolled down the gangway at the end of a cruise? Still the smell of coffee and the discussion of how people like their coffee makes this 'Cruise Ship Creature' easy to identify because where there is coffee then there will be a 'Coffee Connoisseur'.

# CHAPTER 96

## THE EVERYTHING INTOLERANT

The new buzz word sweeping the cruise industry is 'intolerance'.

Note: A general intolerance to idiots never seems to be listed on menus and it should be. I definitely suffer from idiot intolerance. Anyway, I deviate from the intolerance focus.

Before guests take part on a cruise there is often some pre-material to fill in stating whether you have food intolerances. Ships do not want to feed you something that will involve death at the dining table because there isn't that much room in the morgue. Of course death at the dining table is likely due to the general age of cruisers, although no one wants to blame the food. If you are intolerant to nuts, cats, wheat, hedgehogs or dairy then these will not be found in your meal unless there is a massive mistake and of course there will be all manner of compensation claim. 'I clearly stated that I was intolerant to hedgehog and somehow one turned up in my dinner, I demand to see the Hotel Manager because I am deeply insulted.'

Admittedly some people take great pleasure in sharing their intolerance misfortune. At one Officer's table a woman listed all the food she was intolerant to including shellfish, nuts, garlic, dairy, wheat and so many more. I studied her plate and she had a pile of spinach, tomatoes and grilled chicken. For desert she had special jelly. It was no surprise that her diet kept her very lean. During the dinner she delighted in telling us how intolerant she was to certain foods and even screamed when a plate containing oysters passed by. There was a lot of hand flapping and some deep recovery breath. It was an amazing reaction to an oyster. It would be interesting to witness how she would fare with snails. When I asked her what would happen to her if an oyster had launched itself from the plate and clearly grabbed her by the throat she responded that she would come up in a rash. I then quizzed further and discovered that the wheat, the dairy and the shellfish made her stomach bloat. The arm flapping to me had suggested that one misplaced oyster may well end her existence with an internal detonation. She explained that only happened to people who were allergic. Now that would be a whole new concern. 'Detonation on deck 5 – someone was intolerant to an idiot!'

# CHAPTER 97

## THE GIN-A-LING-A-DING-DONGS

Many a gincident has been reported by the 'Gin-A-Ling-A-Ding-Dongs' who generally seem to be the most happily wasted cruisers around the ship. To make the matter increasingly exciting is that there are gin tasting events that attract these specific 'Cruise Ship Creatures' together in one place to sample the joyous gin creations.

After a few gin tasting-tastic moments the group seem to evolve into general hilarity with their crimson cheeks and the hint of blue at the end of their noses. The gin phenomenon catalyses the shyest cruisers to transform into self-professed entertainers and they can be discovered dominating the late night karaoke scene. Others take to the casino tables for a bit of a flutter or even dominate the dance floor with moves and shapes likened to YMCA on speed; although, the shapes will more likely spell G I N. Ever tried creating a recognisable capital N with your body? It is worth a try.

As with all things gin there are many a gincident to report and fantastic moments of congers taking place when there is no actual conger music. One of the best shippy gincidents involved a group of older 'Gin-A-Ling-A-Ding-Dongs' reaching the point of being grievous-ginily-sloshed and deciding that skinny dipping in the central pool at the buffet-face-stuffing peak time was a particularly good idea. Unfortunately, some of the sights floating on the surface was enough to turn carnivores vegetarian, vegetarians, and vegans to breathitarians. When it came to dessert many of the horrified onlookers realised that a moment on the lips could result in the sight of fleshy-nakedness before them. Of course the complainers found the scene disgusting and it definitely ruined their cruise. Security, accompanied by numerous Officers, were called to extract the blighters from the pool. The gincident resulted in the Captain making an announcement stating that under no circumstances were any guests to enter the pool without adequate swimming attire. What absolute gin-ilarity!

# CHAPTER 98

## THE 'LET'S GET SHIT-FACED'

Talking of alcohol... 'Madam, dancing on the table in a dress and forgetting to wear knickers is not appropriate behaviour. Please step down.' The guest was somewhat shit-faced. It was one of those party cruises where the clientele had purchased a cheap four night cruise and their attitude was let's get completely wasted. Oh yes and wasted they were. From the moment they stepped on the ship they were drinking. Cruises like that are the Security section's worst nightmare and the casino's dream. The casino revenue spikes, the takings in the bar sky-rocket and the disco goes on all night. The day at sea is spent recovering from yet another beery blast that will result in the bar staff working until five in the morning. What is amazing is the marvels that take place: those who have been miraculously healed by alcohol toss aside their walking sticks or scooters and pull shapes on the dance floor that can be likened to contortionistic dad dancing with a hint of general convulsion. Many 'Let's Get Shit-faced' shimmy optimistically into the disco with the intention of doing the dance floor caterpillar. It is then the beauty of the reverse evolution reveals itself in the form of the new dance move: 'The Slug!' Splat!

When it comes to ports there is a stagger on mass as they swagger off the gangway to the nearest Duty Free shops where more of the sozzling soda is purchased for tipple-tastic exploration. Most of the alcohol names they can't read but they don't care because sozzle-dom is just a couple of bottles away. Admittedly, it is fascinating to witness wasted piles of people, who have no memory of how they ended up in the pile on deck at 5.30am. With all that in mind: party anyone?

# PART 10

## THE TWO DIFFERENT PERSPECTIVES

Okay so we are nearing the end of the book; so it is worth considering the end of the cruise and how two different mentalities can experience the same cruise very differently. This is a common thing that I noticed on either the last night of the cruise or on the day of disembarkation: perception. It is quite funny how people chat about their cruise experiences as they prepare to leave. Many don't want to go back to real life because they have had a fantastic time. Others just can't be bothered with doing their washing... and... others have a slightly different experience. As I mentioned before – how we filter the world creates our reality... On your last day on a cruise, if you are still spotting 'Cruise Ship Creatures', it is worth paying attention to how people discuss their experience.

## CHAPTER 99

### THE 'YOU'VE TOTALLY RUINED MY CRUISE'

No matter what you do, no matter how much a person can give, there are people who will just never be happy or satisfied. They can be in the most beautiful environment, be fed the most exquisite food and still not enjoy themselves. To make it increasingly bemusing is they find fault in everything and need someone to blame. Unfortunately, what they have not realised is that they themselves are to blame because on all travels you take yourself with you. These people create dramas out of nothing. They somehow manage to walk into situations that you couldn't conceive

187

and these are the people who will be pick-pocketed in the safest port. What you realise is the fact they always look as though there is a smell under their nose or their down-turned mouth reveals that they have never actually managed to turn that frown upside down. There is something about them that just attracts the proverbial shit and in one particular case, this misery ended up having a pipe full of sewage burst behind their cupboard and fill their suitcase with sewage. It was miraculous and if you believe in the law of attraction then you might be suspicious as to what this type of person was thinking about to experience such calamity. In the end these people reach a point where they need to offload and those bony fingers are desperate to point at someone, it is usually reception who are their targets. They will point at the innocent receptionist and scream 'You have totally ruined my cruise.' They will spout on about how many catastrophes have befallen them. A curry has landed in their lap, their wife's hair has turned green, the sewage pipe burst into their suitcase and they have had gastroenteritis. All of that on one cruise and they will never cruise again, it has been terrible, they missed a port and... three months later you see they are on the gangway to experience it all again. Bizarre but true.

# CHAPTER 100

## THE 'YOU'VE TOTALLY MADE MY CRUISE'

At the other end of the cruising scale are the people who just have a lovely time. Everything is fantastic and they can't fault the experience because they aren't focused on finding fault. In fact, they loved every moment. The whole experience was bliss. It doesn't matter that they can't fit into any clothing because the cruising experience was wonderful. So much so they just have to buy a Captain's bloody hat! They have been to some beautiful places, met some fantastic people and were even given super-deluxe fluffy bathrobes. Everything about their whole experience has exhilarated them, the food has astounded them and they have enjoyed being looked after and served. These people have been on the same cruise as the others yet their perception is totally different. They write letters of gratitude and thank the Officers and crew personally. They even say 'You really made my cruise.' With that in mind, maybe it is worth considering who the Officers and crew will go out of their way for, go above and beyond for... Yep you guessed it - the happy, cheerful people who love every moment. These cruisey creatures are valued and loved. They make it very worthwhile to endure seventy hour weeks for a whole contract.

CHAPTER 101


A FEW FINAL WORDS


This book came about because when I returned from my shippy travels I would share some of the more random stories with friends. People always said to me I should write a book on cruising adventures. Have you noticed how many people say 'You should...'? The truth is I loved my time working on ships; however, the hours became too much and my tolerance level dropped to the point where my general love for humanity began to diminish. There were times at three in the morning when you are called to do a helicopter evacuation and your role is to keep corridors clear so that some bugger does not use flash photography that could distract the helicopter pilot and cause the helicopter to crash into the ship and kill everyone. You stand there in your uniform, in an exhausted state knowing you have twelve hours work to complete the next day and you think 'What am I doing...' yet that afternoon in a haze of delirium you could be jet-skiing in some random lagoon surrounded by palm trees somewhere in the Caribbean. When you work on cruise ships every day is the opportunity to live that day to the full never knowing what adventure you are going to stumble upon. What made the gruelling hours bearable was how wonderful the fellow crew were. A community of international people working in their specific roles supporting each other every day. It is such a unique environment and one that I am so grateful to have experienced. So this little compilation was written to remind myself of all the bizarre and beautiful cruisy creatures I observed during my travels and for all those crew who will have witnessed possibly weirder situations than I have written here. Thank you all. My experience on ships was amazing and thank you to all you brilliant guests who have provided me with a whole book of writing material! Please enjoy!

## CHAPTER 102

## CRUISEY, BOOSIE AND A NICE LITTLE REVIEWEY...

If you enjoyed 'Cruise Ship Creatures', then please let your friends know by any means possible. Also it would be wonderful to have your opinion in the form of a review. Thank you so much.

## CHAPTER 103

OTHER BOOKS BY RUBY ALLURE AND MICHELLE DRY

Adult: The Office Zoo – A Field Guide to Office Animal Observation

Love Hunt I – Dating Game. A Kiss and Email Romantic Comedy

Love Hunt II – The Love Game

CLAN DESTINE – Dead Women Have Vendettas

Retina Blue

Money Farm

Teenage: The Resonance

Children's books by Michelle Dry:

Tingle Dingle and The Little Mischiefs

Tingle Dingle and The Treasure Tree

Tingle Dingle and The Land of Boredooom!

The Hairy-Legged Mystery

Elora – The One Winged Fairy and The Last Baby Giggle

Gargantuan Adventures – The Secret Gate

Wyld – One Mammoth Adventure


Non-Fiction:  A Short Course In Creative Writing